Writings of a
Deliberate Agrarian

*One Man's Ruminations About Faith,
Family, and Livin' The Good Life*

HERRICK KIMBALL

FIRST EDITION

WRITINGS OF A DELIBERATE AGRARIAN
Copyright © 2006 by Herrick Kimball

Published by:
Whizbang Books, P.O. Box 1117, Moravia, N.Y. 13118
e-mail: whizbangbooks@bci.net
www.TheDeliberateAgrarian.com

First Printing, 2006
Printed in the United States of America

ISBN: 0-9726564-7-2

Cover design by Laura Coburn
Edited by Carmon Friedrich

Unless otherwise noted, scripture quotations are from the King James Bible.

Dedicated to

Percy Orlan Philbrick
1896 — 1971

---

*He was my grandfather. He was
the greatest agrarian I've ever known.
He is the man pictured with me
(at two years old) on the cover of this book.*

*Make it your ambition to lead a quiet life,
to mind your own business and to work
with your hands, just as we told you,
so that your daily life may win the respect
of outsiders and so that you will not
be dependent on anybody.*

—1 Thessalonians 4:11-12
(New International Version)

Contents

Foreword

WHO AM I THAT I SHOULD WRITE A BOOK about myself, my family, and my beliefs about what makes a good life? That's the question I asked myself when the idea for this little volume first entered my mind. I am, after all, not a highly educated and credentialed expert on the subject. I'm just a regular guy. So I was initially hesitant about putting my writings in book form. But the idea persisted.

Then one day, while mulling it over, it occurred to me that I did not need to approach the writing of this book like I was some sort of authority or expert. Instead, I could simply write it from the viewpoint of a hungry beggar who has discovered a source of bread and wishes to share it with others like himself. I believe that little revelation was God-inspired, and it provided the clarity I needed to bring this book to fruition.

So, my fellow beggars, listen to me . . . I've found bread! And it's not just any old bread. It's good bread. It's bread of the most wholesome, satisfying, and fulfilling kind. It's called Christian agrarian life and culture. Some people call it biblical agrarianism.

Perhaps you have never heard the term "Christian agrarian" before. If not, let me assure you that this concept is nothing new. Fact is, it's so old that its roots reach all the way back to the beginning of recorded time, when God Himself planted a garden in Eden (Genesis 2:8). Then He put the man, Adam, in His garden and told him to "tend it and keep it" (Genesis 2:15).

Christian agrarians today believe that the fundamental corporate calling of mankind has not changed since Genesis. They believe that biblical culture and agrarian culture are (or should be) the same thing. In other words, they believe the fullness of Christian life is best lived within agrarianism.

Agriculture—the cultivation of the earth and animals to produce food—is fundamental to what it means to be an agrarian. That isn't to say that all agrarians are farmers, because most are not, especially nowadays. But agrarian sentiments naturally translate into a desire to cultivate and care for a section of land: to make it fruitful, to draw sustenance from it. Christian agrarians believe the stewardship of creation is one of their God-ordained responsibilities.

Closely related to the act of producing food is the agrarian's reverence for creation in its many forms. Christian agrarians in particular recognize the beauty, the incredible complexity, and the reliable order seen in the natural world as the handiwork of an awesome Creator—clear evidence of the great and holy God they worship.

These days, many modern Christians are seeking to rediscover traditional understandings about agrarian life—concepts that have largely vanished over two centuries of industrialization and corporate domination.

For example, the interconnected relationships and dependencies between land, family, local community, and the local church, which were once so strong and central to the everyday existence of godly people, have virtually disappeared in our modern age. Christian agrarians desire to reestablish those relationships. They want to build a healthy, wholesome, sustainable, and God-honoring agrarian culture in the midst of the God-hating popular culture that has none of those qualities. Such a way of life, founded on faith, family, work, and charity, would be (as it has always shown itself to be) a wellspring of virtue, a testament to the power of lives transformed by the Spirit of the Lord.

The key to restoring those lost ideals of vibrant agrarian culture is the restoration of vibrant families. With that in mind, Christian agrarians are deliberately retaking functions of the home and family that have been lost to the industrial malaise. Home birth and home education have been bellwether movements, not commonly understood to be agrarian but, nevertheless, fitting perfectly into the agrarian ideal.

Our modern culture demands that people strive and invest huge amounts of time away from their homes and families to achieve material success and comfort, and this has weakened the family. With that sobering reality in mind, Christian agrarian fathers and mothers are forsaking materialistic definitions of success. They are turning their hearts toward home and investing more time in family-centered pursuits. They are re-embracing traditional roles and biblical responsibilities. They are delighting in the fruit of the womb and, as the Lord blesses, having larger families.

The typical Christian agrarian family eschews pointless busyness and consumerism in favor of wise self-denial, simplicity, and domestic productivity. Homemaking skills are cultivated and valued. Craftsmanship is honored. Self-sufficiency is practiced. Family bonds are strengthened when all members of the family work together to provide for its sustenance.

Those who understand Christian agrarianism understand that it is, ultimately, a multigenerational vision of cultural reformation. Families are agents of positive social change, not in the modern, special interest, political sense, but in the biblical sense, the sense that grows out of Jesus Christ's command to forgive, and to love your neighbor. Such families are like blocks of solid granite in the foundation of this new social order.

There are some Christian sects that have always been and continue to be agrarian. The Amish and Mennonites come to mind. But Christian agrarians, as I've endeavored to define them here, are people who, like myself, are part of

3

mainstream Christian denominations. We do not claim any special revelation, just a special conviction. We are nothing more and nothing less than children of the King who desire to bring glory to Him through the lives we lead.

I believe that Christianity and agrarianism go together like a carefully planted seed and rich soil. I also believe that when Christians seek to understand agrarianism with humility and honesty, the Holy Spirit will convict, and positive change will result. That is why I have published the essays in this book. My writings are a personal testament and a gentle apologetic for Christian agrarianism. This book is not, by any means, the whole story on this subject. It is more like several teaspoon samples of a much larger feast.

Finally, I would like to point out that Christian agrarianism is something so simple and wise that, in the midst of our complicated modern culture, it stands out as truly remarkable. And since it has the power to change lives, it is, by definition, revolutionary.

With that in mind, welcome to the revolution . . . .

*Agrarianism is the only proper seedbed
of a Christian life and worldview.
The whole Bible teaches it,
and every story and parable re-affirms it.*
—Michael Bunker
Towards a Biblical/Agrarian Culture

*Agricultural communities, where the
brotherhoods of labor and cooperation bring
about increased understanding, provide
a potential model for an ideal social order.*
—M. Thomas Inge
Agrarianism in American Literature

4

Introduction

I AM AN AGRARIAN. SPECIFICALLY, I AM A Christian agrarian. I believe that God intended for His people to live their lives and raise their families for His glory within an agrarian paradigm.

That is why my wife, Marlene, and I eschew the city and live out in the countryside. That is why we homeschool our three boys, ages 11 to 17. That is why we teach our children to acknowledge the Sovereign Lord of All Creation as the Sovereign Lord of All Creation. That is why we look to His grace every day and give thanks for the good times as well as the hard times (also known as the teaching times). That is why we have a garden. That is why we keep hens for eggs. That is why we heat our house with a woodstove. That is why we make our own maple syrup. That is why we grind wheat "berries" into flour, from which Marlene makes the best homemade breads that you'll ever taste.

We do these things and more because we are aspiring to live within that agrarian paradigm.

This framework for living, this kind of work, can make life richer. If pursued with humility and wisdom, in a spirit of love, this is the kind of life that can make a family strong and be a remarkable witness to the goodness of a merciful God.

To live this kind of life is to be a blessing to the community around you in the here-and-now, and to bless the generations that will follow you. This kind of life is a beacon of light amidst the pervasive shallow, false promises of the dying industrial culture in which we live. It is a way of life that, very simply, offers hope, peace, and contentment like nothing else.

Here I am, a simple rural man, beginning these ruminations sounding like a philosopher! You know, I think that's entirely appropriate for a Deliberate Agrarian. Fortunately, for one who is not a particularly deep thinker, like myself, the precious riches of this "philosophy" can be clearly seen and easily grasped—and they sparkle brightly.

If you have not already done so, I invite you, dear reader, to seek and discover some of these treasures for yourself. But first, let me share with you in the following pages a little about the life, work, hope, struggles, lessons, thoughts, prayers, and blessings that have come into the life and times of this Deliberate Agrarian.

It is my great desire that you will be inspired and blessed along the way.

Yes, I am positive that
one of the great curatives
of our evils, our maladies,
social, moral, and intellectual,
would be a return to the soil,
a rehabilitation of the work of the fields.
—Charles Wagner

I

The Breakfast of Agrarians

THERE ARE ALL KINDS OF GOOD FOODS THAT agrarians can eat for breakfast.

Eggs come to mind right away. I'm not referring to those perfectly uniform, perfectly clean, perfectly prosaic eggs found *en masse* at the supermarket, the ones with pale, flat yolks and watery whites, laid by chickens which have never seen the light of day, let alone scratched in the dirt and eaten an insect, or swallowed a genuine stone for their gizzard, but real eggs, laid by down-to-earth country hens, eggs that come out of the nest in a variety of sizes, with a variety of imperfections, and sometimes a smear of wet soil (from a muddy hen's foot) or, horror of horrors, a spot of manure. Fresh from the nest are best.

Bacon is good, too, as is sausage. Homemade bread, toasted, with some real butter, and perhaps some fruit preserves, is also a fine agrarian breakfast food.

My grandfather Philbrick, a potato farmer in northern Maine, would often go just up the road, in the dawn of the day, to catch his morning's meal in the stream. He loved pan-fried brook trout for breakfast.

Yes, there are plenty of hale and hearty breakfast foods from which agrarians may choose. But there is also lots of morning fare that agrarians will not eat, such as the vast majority of breakfast foods found in a modern supermarket. Froot Loops and Lucky Charms come to mind, as do Pop Tarts, pseudo-juice drinks, white "Wonder" bread, nondairy dairy products, and anything labeled "fortified with nine vitamins plus iron."

I understand you can even buy egg substitutes now: eggs without the shells and, for that matter, eggs without the egg. It is remarkable, really, the myriad ways the industrial providers can morph natural food into something unnatural or—worse yet—a synthesized copy.

This fare of the industrial providers is food foolishness. These people, these companies, these forces, exalt themselves and their fake products, boldly proclaiming that their creations are better than the unadulterated bounty created and provided by the Sovereign God of all creation. What gall!

I had a perfect agrarian breakfast a few days ago. It was the exact breakfast that prompted me to write this story.

The first thing you need to know about this particular breakfast (for it is no small matter) is that it was made for me by a particularly special person—my loving wife, Marlene.

Picture in your mind a bowl of oatmeal—that is where we will begin. No, not that cook-it-in-the-microwave-in-3.7-seconds oatmeal, the stuff that comes in little prepackaged envelopes, complete with processed white sugar (or brown, which is white with something else added to make it brown), artificial flavors, and special chemicals to preserve freshness.

I'm speaking of oatmeal that consists of nothing more than rolled oats: the flattened flakes that result when oat kernels are run through steel rollers, the kind of oatmeal that requires a couple pinches of salt and several minutes of cooking on the stovetop.

This bowl of oatmeal I ate the other day was cooked to "Baby Bear" perfection: not too hot, not too cold, not soupy, not lumpy—it was just right.

To sweeten this heavenly bowl of cooked grain, Marlene poured on some maple syrup. *Aunt Jemima's* is my favorite! Okay, so I'm being sarcastic. The maple syrup on my oatmeal was not factory-made, caramel-colored sugar syrup, it was one hundred percent boiled-down sugar maple tree sap. I know this because my family and I tapped the trees, gathered the sap, and cooked it down over a wood fire in our back yard. No sweetener on earth can compare to the amber nectar that is real maple syrup.

Marlene then poured just a little cream over the oatmeal. The cream came from Esther Thornton's cow. I think it is a Guernsey. Twice a week, we get fresh milk from Esther's cow. The thick, rich cream rises to the top of the container and we skim it off. Cream just doesn't get much better than that.

Next, my dear wife added a small handful of walnuts. These were store-bought halves, but I'm quite certain they were the real thing. It's hard to mess up walnuts. But just give 'em time; I'm sure there are scientists all over the world working to create an artificial substitute for tree-grown nutmeat, cracked out of its hard shell. Whoever achieves this noble goal will be fêted as a hero by the industrial providers. Maybe he or she will win a big prize. Most importantly, though, they will get rich! Whatever.

There was one more element to my breakfast. It was, as the French say, the *pièce de résistance*: fresh strawberries.

Only moments before, Marlene had carefully selected a couple dozen plump, dew-speckled, sun-ripened, melt-in-your-mouth-sweet berries. They came right from our garden. These deep crimson beauties were rinsed, hulled, sliced in half, and piled on a small plate beside my bowl of oatmeal. They were there for me to eat in whatever way pleased me; I could have them in my oatmeal (which I did), or I could eat them individually (which I also did).

I didn't eat this meal right away. I sat and marveled at it. I felt as if I were a great agrarian king . . . king over the 1.5 acre dominion that God has granted to me. I gave Him thanks for the simple, yet wholly indescribable, beauty of the bounty that I was about to receive.

Amen.

9

Earth's crammed with heaven
And every common bush afire with God;
But only he who sees, takes off his shoes-
The rest sit around and pluck blackberries.
—Elizabeth Barrett Browning

❦

Oh, Adam was a gardener,
And God who made him sees
That half a proper gardener's work
Is done upon his knees.
—Rudyard Kipling

❦

The kiss of the sun for pardon,
The song of the birds for mirth,
One is nearer God's heart in a garden
Than anywhere else on earth.
—Dorothy Frances Gurney

❦

Sowe carrets in your gardens,
and humbly praise God for them,
as for a singular and great blessing.
—Richard Gardiner (1599)

❦

To own a bit of ground, to scratch it with a hoe,
to plant seeds and watch their renewal of life-
this is the commonest delight of the race,
the most satisfactory thing a man can do.
—Charles Dudley Warner

2

An Episode
of Garden Repose

M Y GARDEN PRINCIPALLY CONSISTS OF 24 beds. Each bed measures 4 ft. by 8 ft. and each is a small, manageable field where crops, or combinations of crops, are planted intensively. The soil in the beds is a sandy loam, fertile from steady applications of homemade compost over the years. Between the beds is a walkway. Each walkway is carpeted with a thick layer of oat straw. The straw serves as a mulch to keep moisture in the ground and weeds from germinating.

Morning before last, I was in my garden thinning a bed of carrots. The tops are now around 8 in. high. The many rows are 4 ft. long and spaced 10 in. apart. I am thinning the carrots so that I have one approximately every 6-inches in the rows. It is tedious work but I enjoy it. I enjoy having my bare hands in the soil. I enjoy having the earth under my fingernails and the pores of my fingers stained chlorophyll green.

But I am tired this morning. Friends were over last night. Old friends. Comfortable friends. We sat under the stars around a fire, on the lawn, not far from my garden. We talked of our families, of our memories, of our dreams and plans, and even of our gardens. We talked late into the night. It was good to visit like that. We should do it more often. But I seldom stay up so late, and I am tired this morning. Thinning carrots is a good thing to do when you are tired.

The straw beckons me. First, I sit. Then I lay down. It is surprisingly comfortable. It is even more comfortable than my bed. My legs are stretched right out, ankles crossed. My arms are bent at the elbows, with my palms like a pillow under my head. My lower back, a little sore before, now feels good. Very good, indeed.

I close my eyes and rest. Time passes. I am unaware that Marlene, my wife, is over beyond the garden, walking to the hen house. I hear her voice in the distance: "Are you okay?"

I respond: "Yep."

I think to myself that if I lived in a populated place, like the suburbs, and I was lying on the ground like this, people would be alarmed. Of course, it is normal for people to lie on a beach, but I am in my garden. Men do not recline on the earth like this unless they are physically sick, or, perhaps, mentally ill. An ambulance or police car might arrive on the scene. I might be taken away for closer examination.

It is a bright, but overcast, morning. The clouds are fluffy and dense. I open my eyes and gaze straight up, through my sunglasses. But I do not see any clouds. I see continents. I am looking down from the heavens. These foreign lands are milk-white and dapple-gray against the bright blue oceans. There are all manner of geographical phenomena: ragged coastlines, curled capes, frilly firths, and islands, islands all about. How remarkable.

Marlene walks over. She is wearing a yellow apron and has four fresh, brown-shelled eggs in her hand. "Aren't you afraid you'll get 'buggy' laying there like that?"

I am a little concerned, but I say, "Nope." She tells me she is very tired, too. We talk a few moments and she walks towards the house.

I put my knees up so the soles of my feet are flat on the ground. I interlock my fingers over my chest, and look back down. The continents have moved. New lands have appeared. They did not look as though they were in motion before. I study, trying to discern movement, but I can not see it. I do, however, see a pair of swallows glide across my field of view. Down lower, I see and hear an occasional fly as it zips to who-knows-where. Amazingly, the flies are not bothering me.

There is a sound to my left in the walkway on the other side of my field of carrots. I turn my head to see and there is a young Cornish hen; it's one of my meat birds. She is half the size of the males her age. This critter escaped her pen a little while ago when I moved it to fresh grass. I often let these lucky ones roam and glean for awhile before returning them to the caged flock.

Miss Chicken has no manners. She enters my carrot field, walking across the rows, stepping right on the greens in her little chicken quest. She is oblivious to the intelligent design and work of my hands here. Her focus is to find another tidbit that will momentarily satisfy her constant longing for fulfillment. She does not know that in another four weeks she will be in my freezer.

The creature makes her way towards me, her head bobbing forward and backward with the steps. She stops momentarily along the way to peck at every morsel that strikes her fancy. Her legs and feet are not wan, like those of factory-raised birds; they are bright orange. Her feathers are white and clean. Her eyes are bright. Her beak is dirty.

Now within a foot of my face, the curious creature cranes her neck, looking at me with one eye, like chickens do. I realize she must see her reflection in my sunglasses. Will she peck?

I grin and, with my best English gardener brogue exclaim, "My, but you're a silly bird, aren't you?" She retracts her head and walks away, bobbing and searching, searching, always searching.

There is something crawling on my forearm. I lift my arm up and see a small ant struggling to traverse the hairy terrain. I bring my arm closer to see better (I am of the age that I must now look over my glasses to see up close), but my study is promptly cut short; the tiny insect has lost its footing and fallen on my white t-shirt. I brush it off and roll on my left side, facing the carrots. My bicep and bent arm are now the pillow. My right arm is at my side. I am looking at my garden from the vantage of a woodchuck or, considering the carrot greens, perhaps a rabbit. How many people have viewed their garden from this position? It is fascinating.

I see beauty I've never beheld before. The unthinned carrot rows arch over loamy Main Streets like majestic elm trees once did in long-ago New England villages. In the distance, beyond the dark broccoli forest, there is a wisp of white smoke, the lingering remnant of last evening's fellowship. The bed of cantaloupe vines reminds me of an impenetrable Amazon rain forest. A lone bumblebee is being her busy self, sampling every freshly-opened blossom of my two-year-old lavender plants. Yes, I have planted lavender in my vegetable garden. I do not eat it; it does not serve to fill my stomach. I smell the blossoms, and I look at the delicate beauty of this plant because it fills my senses and my soul with wonder.

I look at my watch. I have been lying here in my garden for nearly 45 minutes. Rolling to my back, I resolve to stay here for another 15 minutes, then close my eyes, resting. The cloud cover has moved. The sun's rays are warming my face.

It has been a sweet repose, a rare experience. I think to myself that I should do it more often. But I've also started thinking of other things, of the work I want to get done this day in my workshop. I have obligations. The carrots can wait. I feel refreshed, renewed, and I get up.

Now, where did that little chicken go?

The grower of trees, the gardener,
the man born to farming,
whose hands reach into the ground
and sprout, to him the soil is a divine drug.
He enters into death yearly, and comes back
rejoicing. He has seen the light lie down in
the dung heap, and rise again in the corn.
—Wendell Berry
The Man Born To Farming

3

My Debt-Free Home and a Personal Testimony

WHEN MARLENE AND I MARRIED IN 1980, we moved into a two-room apartment on a side street in the village of Moravia, New York, I was 22, she was 21. We had done some college and had recently gotten full-time jobs. I worked for a local contractor doing things like barn repair and roofing. Marlene was a secretary for a doctor in town.

She made more money than I did, but neither of us had high-paying jobs. We lived as cheaply as we could. Our goal was to save up enough money to buy a piece of land. After a couple years, we had saved a few thousand dollars, so we started looking for just the right piece of property. We hunted for a small parcel of land. A couple acres would do, preferably with some woods, some tillable, and some privacy. We wanted to build a house that would be a home and to have a big garden. Our dreams were simple and agrarian.

We looked at several potential places before finally setting our sights on one corner of an alfalfa field on a gently-sloping hillside. The location was about three miles from my parent's house and six miles from Marlene's parents. There was woodland on one side and in the back, and fields everywhere else. A beautiful, fast-flowing stream ran through the woods. There was only one house in sight up the road. I knew the property owner and mentioned my interest in his land to him. He said he would think about it.

Some time passed and the owner called. He would sell us 1.5 acres for $2,500. We had the money. We bought it. As soon as the papers were signed and the checks were written and the hands were shaken, we went to our land and rejoiced. *Our* land. The land God had blessed us with. It was a special thing. A great goal had been achieved.

We spent a lot of time on our land. I built a small equipment shed, bought a rototiller, planted a big garden and some apple trees and raspberry bushes. We talked about the dream home we wanted to build. The only problem was that we had virtually no money to build a house.

Most people, when they want to build a house and do not have the money, will go to a bank for a loan. I would not do that. It was out of the question. I have this thing about banks: I don't like them. I had read and heard too many stories about banks taking people's homes away from them during the Great Depression of the 1930s. My parents had suffered with financial problems over the years which also affected my attitudes about debt.

We bought property we could afford to pay cash for because I wanted the security and freedom that comes with owning a piece of land outright. Mortgaging it to a bank would be going against some very strongly-held convictions. I told Marlene that I would rather live in a shack on a piece of land that we owned free and clear than in a nice house that the bank owned. And I meant it.

So I looked into all kinds of alternative housing options, including yurts, the traditional dwellings of Mongolian herdsmen. I think yurts are really neat. They're better than tipis. Marlene was not as enthusiastic as I about living in a yurt. She suggested that her dad might lend us some money.

Jay W. Myers was my father-in-law (he is now deceased). When I married his little girl, the youngest of his six children, he was retired from dairy farming, had sold his farm, and kept busy with a little business trucking cattle for area farmers. Jay and his wife, Evelyn (who was 42 when Marlene was born), were married during the Depression. They started out with nothing. They knew hardship. And like most everyone who lived through those lean years, they were frugal people. Jay was able to loan us $10,000. We paid it back with interest in five years, never missing a payment.

With that money and a lot of work we built a decent little house. It measured only 16 ft. by 24 ft. The upstairs had a bedroom and a bathroom and a landing at the top where a washer and dryer could someday go. Downstairs was a kitchen and a living room. There was also a 10 ft. by 10 ft. one-story attachment on the lower level that gave us an entryway and some extra room in the kitchen. A wood stove in the living room was, and still is, our only source of heat. Our well was a 12 ft. deep hole in the ground, dug by a backhoe and lined with concrete blocks. There was no basement; the house was built on concrete piers. We mixed the concrete in an old rusty mixer we found in the hedgerow behind Jay's house. Some of the windows were recycled, some were inexpensive single-pane barn sashes. The inside staircase was salvaged from an old camp.

We spent three years building our house nights, weekends, and vacations while working our regular jobs. During this time, we moved out of our little apartment and lived with Jay and Evelyn. This allowed us to save the $155 a month we had been paying for rent, not to mention the cost of food and utilities. It puts a lump in my throat now to think how Marlene's parents helped us out back then. They did not give us money, but they gave us a legitimate loan and let us live with them for a season. It was never a problem living with my in-laws—it was a tremendous blessing.

We moved into our house before it was finished, and our first child was born thereafter. Marlene quit her job to be a full-time mother. It was a challenge living on my one income. There was no extra money to finish the loose ends on the house, and with the new baby, our once-cozy abode was getting cramped. We made do until our next baby arrived three years later, and I had to make the house bigger. There was some savings, but not much. Back we went to Jay. Our credit was good. He loaned us another $10,000.

I put a 16 ft. by 20 ft. addition on where the 10 ft. by 10 ft. entry had been. That gave us a big bedroom upstairs and a back room off the kitchen. I also put a basement under the addition. The money ran out before the work was done. Forget siding. Tar paper over plywood would do, and to this day, I still need to put siding on the back of my house.

God blessed us with a third son. The demands of working to provide for my growing family meant that I did not work much on the house for several years. During this time, I went into business for myself as a small-scale, hands-on remodeling contractor, and I borrowed another $10,000 from Jay to build a garage-size workshop in the yard not far from the house. It was finished on the outside, but the house was not.

My work as a contractor was all-consuming. I invested an incredible amount of time and energy into the business. It was that way for ten years. I did not have much of a garden while I was growing my business. The apple trees I planted did not get pruned, the raspberry patch died off. I barely had time to mow the lawn. Money was tight. Marlene would sometimes suggest that she could go back to work part time to help out. I was adamant that this would not happen. We did not have much, but at the very least, my children would have a full-time mother, a conviction of mine that is more strongly held than that of not borrowing money from a bank. We would make do. The Lord would provide.

And He did provide. My grandmother gifted some money to us on two occasions. It was not a huge amount, but it was enough to take the pressure off and make a huge difference. We were always careful with our money. We bought used vehicles and drove them until they were high-mileage junkers. We did not buy anything on a credit card that we could not pay off at the end of the month. We kept our bills paid and saved what we could for the proverbial rainy day. We also managed to pay off our loans from Jay.

Starting around 1998, that proverbial rainy day came. A series of circumstances left me discouraged, burnt-out, on the verge of serious depression, and broke. God was dealing with me. What savings we had dwindled to nothing. I cashed in my retirement IRA. I borrowed everything I could on my life insurance policy. There was only $250 left in my checking account. Jay was not around to borrow from. The only thing I had left of material value was my home and the land. It was paid for. I could get a home equity loan . . . if I went to a bank.

Yes, indeed, when He wants to, God sure knows how to get our attention and bring us to our knees in humility and repentance. The Bible says that He chastises those whom He loves. I haven't a doubt in my mind that He was chastising me, and I know for a fact that He loves me. I came out of that valley of despair and confusion with a healthy fear of the Lord. I came to realize, in a tangible way, that He is sovereign and I am not. That time of sorrows gave me a whole new perspective about my life, about what is most important, about what I needed to be doing.

I did not have to go to the bank. God blessed and provided just enough to get me back on track, and He directed me into a new line of work. It is less stressful, less consuming. It pays the bills, giving a little extra for saving. It is not a job I particularly like, because it takes me away from my family each day. But I am thankful for it, and it is where I believe He wants me for now.

There have been other changes too. I started gardening again. I cut down the apple trees, which never yielded well, and planted grapes. We started raising chickens for meat and eggs. I rediscovered the agrarian and homesteading interests of my younger days. I turned my attention more to my family, to being a good father, a good husband, a good example. And last year I got back to working on the house.

19

It is still a small house, and it is a crowded house with three boys in one bedroom. But it is a solid and well-built structure, and it is our home. It is the home that our Father in heaven has given us. This home and the land it rests on is an agrarian haven. It is a place of peace and stability in the midst of a rebellious and disoriented modern world. In this humble home is a family that loves and cares and prays for each other and for those around us. It is a home where God's goodness is understood and acknowledged. It is a home where He is lifted up and glorified.

This is as it should be. I wish that everyone could experience this good life.

Home, the spot of earth supremely blest,
A dearer, sweeter spot than all the rest.
—Robert Montgomery

'Mid pleasures and palaces though we may roam
Be it ever so humble, there's no place like home.
—John Howard Payne

I'd rather be on my farm
than be emperor of the world.
—George Washington

Debt is the worst poverty
—Thomas Fuller (1732)

4

On Picking Strawberries in the Early Morning

L AST YEAR I PLANTED TWO 50 FT. ROWS OF strawberries. One row is *Ozark Beauty* and the other is *Tribute*. They are everbearing varieties. Last week I took a day off from work to pick my strawberries. Well, actually, I took it off for other reasons, but I determined that first thing in the morning I would give the rows a thorough picking.

We have been eating from these rows for over a week. Marlene has made strawberry shortcake, and as I noted in a previous story, strawberries can be an important part of the Breakfast of Agrarians. My boys have also been grazing through the berries.

At first, when I saw them swarming down the rows, I looked upon my sons as juvenile locusts, devouring the fruits of my labor. I felt like I should tell them to stay out. But the Lord spoke to me in that small voice . . . "Didn't you plant those berries so your family could enjoy them? What could be more enjoyable than being a barefoot boy amidst two long rows of ripe strawberries? Look at the beauty of this thing you and I have created."

Before my hasty thoughts and words could do their damage, I came to the realization that through my hard work and God's grace, my sons will have these small, but wonderful and important, childhood memories. Perhaps, one day, these memories will motivate my children to plant strawberries for their families. I sure do hope so.

But sporadic picking of the choicest berries had left a lot of other lesser-but-still-good fruit, and it needed to be thoroughly picked. So there I was, shortly after five o'clock in the morning, on my hands and knees in the dew-wet straw mulch, deliberately scrutinizing every single berry.

I was working in those fresh, special moments of the morning when the summer sun is rising, bright and warm, but the air is still cool from the previous evening. It's a time that the Moderns miss because they are still sleeping or just not paying attention, and frankly, they couldn't care less about it.

Some of the perfectly ripe berries make a distinct, audible snap as I tug them from the stem. It is a sound I've heard in seasons past, but I had forgotten. I also pick the overripe berries. These are distinguished by their lack of sheen (a ripe berry reflects the sun; you might say it sparkles) and are tossed onto the lawn. I do the same with berries that have been gnawed by slugs. Occasionally, I run across gruesome blackened berries, covered with white, powdery mold. I break these off further up the stem and toss them away with extra vigor.

My big stainless steel bowl fills. Morning grogginess is quickly melting away. Garden work always vitalizes me; it makes me feel more alive.

I am conscious of the sounds around me, mostly bird sounds. Songbirds are in full chorus. My Cornish broilers, in their cage on the front lawn, are peeping excitedly because I moved them to fresh grass. Hens cackle away out behind my workshop. I can hear the water in the shale-bottomed creek behind my house as it rushes over a series of short water-falls on its way to Owasco Lake. My dog's collar tags jingle as she lays, feet up, on the road, twisting her torso, scratching her back on the coarse blacktop. Her name is Annie.

I concentrate on listening "deep". . . in the valley below I can hear an occasional big truck barreling down the State Road. That's it for audible evidence of any other humans until, after a half-hour of picking, I hear a familiar morning sound. It is the muffled thud of kitchen cupboard doors closing shut inside my house. Marlene has gotten up and is starting her day. A short while later, I hear the house door open. Annie's head perks and she looks expectantly. We both know Marlene is coming out to see us.

Marlene is wearing lavender-colored pajamas, white sandals, and "movie star" sunglasses. A damp dish towel is slung over one shoulder. She smiles that intoxicatingly sweet smile that attracted me to her many years ago when we were just teenagers. It still does. I count this woman as one of God's greatest blessings in my life.

It has been forty minutes since I started picking berries. I am now moving from the *Tribute* row to the *Ozark Beauty*. My neighbor's pickup truck speeds down the road. He lives a couple miles away and works as a self-employed concrete mason. It is the first vehicle to go by since I started picking.

The *Ozark Beauty* plants are visibly different from the *Tribute*. Their foliage is far more lush and attractive, but they bear far less fruit than the *Tribute*. It occurs to me that some people are like *Ozark Beauty* strawberry plants.

After about an hour I have picked both rows. Two more vehicles motor by before I finish. A chain saw comes to life somewhere in the way-off distance. I end up with two good-size bowls of berries, the delicious fruits of my labor.

Washing, hulling, and slicing the berries for freezing takes me another hour. I end up with five ziplock quart bags full. They will be saved and cherished in winter shortcakes and smoothies. I feel very good about what I've accomplished. More berries will be ready for picking in a couple of days.

Moderns can't help but do the math: two hours of work to prepare five packages of frozen strawberries . . . "Wow! Those are some expensive berries you got there! Don't you agrarians realize it's cheaper and easier to just go buy frozen fruit at the supermarket? "

That is the natural conclusion of people who live their lives believing that money is the only—or, at least, the most important—standard of value.

Agrarians, on the other hand, see this sort of thing very differently. We see value in the doing of planting, tending, harvesting, processing, and putting up our own food. We see value in knowing where our food comes from. We see value in the assurance that this food is pure and safe. We see value in the incredibly superior flavor of homegrown and fresh-picked food. We see value in the satisfaction that comes with being able to take care of our own food needs and not being dependent on the industrial providers, even if it is just in part. This is freedom. This is part of what makes The Good Life good.

*It is always exciting to open the door and
go out into the garden for the first time on any day.*
—Marion Cran

❦

*Just as a prism of glass miters light and
casts a colored braid, a garden sings sweet
incantations the human heart strains to hear.
Hiding in every flower, in every leaf, in every twig
and bough, are reflections of the God
who once walked with us in Eden.*
—Tonia Triebwasser

❦

*When I go into my garden with a spade,
and dig a bed, I feel such an exhilaration and health
that I discover that I have been defrauding myself
all this time in letting others do for me
what I should have done with my own hands.*
—Ralph Waldo Emerson

❦

*A garden really lives only insofar as it is
an expression of faith, the embodiment of
a hope and a song of praise.*
—Russell Page
The Education of a Gardener

❦

*The satisfying labors of a gardener are among
the most profound and paradoxical
evidences of grace in all of life.*
—John Calvin

5

Moderns
and the Antithesis

I SOMETIMES USE THE WORD "MODERNS" IN MY ruminations. Moderns are a particular kind of people. I should define what kind of people I think these Moderns are. Or, at least, try.

Most people get their definitions from a dictionary. There I found that one meaning of modern is "a person having modern ideas, beliefs, standards, etc." That is a fine definition but I think it is too vague. We really need some specifics.

For example, Moderns are ignorant about where the food they eat comes from and how it is produced. Since the average Modern gets all his food from a grocery store or some form of eatery, he is distanced and disconnected from the original source of production. Moderns like grocery store food because it is processed and ready to eat. And they like it that processors add vitamins and minerals and other enrichments to make the food more "nutritious." As long as all this grocery store food is relatively cheap and plentiful, which it always has been, and as far as they are concerned, always will be, the Moderns are pleased as pigs in mud.

The analogy of pigs and mud is humorous because it is so perfectly contrary to modern sensibilities. The Moderns actually like to have everything in their lives sterile and sanitized. That means farm animals and the places where they live, which inevitably smell like manure, are gross and offensive to the Modern. Mud is wet dirt—"dirt" being the Modern word for "soil"—and dirt is, of course, bad because it is unsanitary. It's full of germs, don't you know?

Moderns do not like to toil in the earth or, for that matter, do any more physical work than they absolutely must. Leisure is one of their primary objectives in life. Why go to all the work of growing food, the Modern reasons, when you can just buy it at the supermarket? Moderns will hire someone to mow their lawns and do other manual yard tasks for them so they can have time to do things that are a whole lot more fun, like playing golf or working out at a health club. Such modern recreational activities are a substitute for the physical benefits of old-fashioned work.

The Moderns look down on those who labor and sweat, those who work close to the earth and out in the elements. Farmers and homesteaders are filthy bumpkins, hayseeds, fodder for jokes. Respectable work to a Modern is a job that does not get you dirty and does not require you to perspire.

Moderns continually need to be entertained by the circus of modern amusements. They are addicted to the visceral and vicarious thrills that come with watching sports or reality television programs or soap operas, or any of the other forms of electronic sewage that emanate from their big screens.

Along these same lines, Moderns crave to know more about the titillating and sordid lives of modern celebrities. The modern media readily feeds the Moderns all this dysfunction in its many forms.

Because they are so tuned into the media of the popular culture and its steady stream of marketing messages, Moderns are conditioned to be materialists. They want the newest and biggest and best of everything. If they are not constantly consuming more industrial goods, they are not happy.

Moderns are also impatient. They want what they want, and they want it NOW! Easy credit was invented to satisfy these constant yearnings. Delayed gratification is not a concept they comprehend.

The materialism of the Moderns naturally leads to dissatisfaction. No matter how much a Modern has, he wants more. Surely, dissatisfaction and discontentment is a universal condition of fallen mankind, affecting more than just the Moderns, but they are consummate experts at it.

Closely tied to this materialism is a one-sided understanding of success. To the Modern, success is measured only in the financial understanding of the word; he who makes the most money and accumulates the most stuff is the biggest success in the eyes of a Modern.

Most Moderns are Malthusians. In their belief system, the fewer children the better. Children are viewed as obstacles to personal success and material prosperity.

For the most part, Moderns reject the idea of one sovereign God and transcendental truth. Instead, they embrace the wisdom and goodness of mankind as embodied in the institutions of education, government, science, and industry. These are where they put their hope and faith. As a result, Moderns are in bondage to these institutions and to corporate-industrial providers. And, just like those wallowing pigs, they like it that way.

There is my definition of the quintessential Modern. I hope I have not offended anyone. My purpose is not to be unkind to Moderns, but to be truthful about the Moderns' world. Sometimes the truth is not pleasant, but it is, nevertheless, the truth, and someone needs to point it out once in awhile.

Sometimes the truth hurts. To paraphrase Pogo, "I have seen the Moderns, and they are me." Perhaps you have noticed within this definition something of yourself, too. I would be very surprised if you didn't.

That is not to say that you and I are therefore Moderns. I know I'm not, and I sure do hope you're not. The distinction lies first in the seeing and then, in the doing. I've lifted the galvanized lid of the modern culture enough to catch a whiff of its decaying rancidity. I've seen and, to an extent, experienced the pride, selfishness, and emptiness. I want nothing of it. Furthermore, I see the dependency, and it alarms me.

I want The Good Life for myself, my family, and my friends. The Good Life I speak of is real gold, not fools' gold or, worse, some ersatz foil veneer over plastic. I'm convinced that this Good Life is best found in Christian agrarian culture. Such culture is the total antithesis of modernism. It is the antidote for modernism's poison.

As a Christian agrarian, I am making a conscious effort (the "doing" I spoke of earlier) to distance myself and my family from the self-destructing culture of the Moderns. That is why I call myself a *Deliberate* Agrarian.

I have made much progress in recent years. I am not at all the Modern I once was. But there is still a long way to go. That is okay, though, because this journey is a good one. As I learn and apply agrarian skills and Christian principles, I am reaping literal and spiritual fruits from my labors. I'm discovering that The Good Life is as much in the journey as it is in the destination. I am on my way, and I'm loving it!

*The moderns will either follow the lead of
Nebuchadnezzer, finally humbling themselves
and acknowledging the one true God, or that of
his son Belshazzar, wallowing in their pride
until God finally strikes them down. In either
case, God will be honored and glorified. The
kingdom of modernity will collapse, and when
the dust subsides and the rubble is cleared away,
we will see the specifics now for what we can
only take on faith—that the rise and fall of
modernity was also part of the Father's plan,
that the foolishness of the world has once again
been weighed in the balance and found wanting,
and the rule of King Jesus will have extended
further than ever.*
—Rick Saenz,
Dry Creek Chronicles

6

Deliberate Contentment

A FEW STORIES BACK I TOLD YOU HOW MAR-
lene and I acquired our land and the home we live
in, and how God has blessed our family. I believe
the agrarian life we experience here is truly idyllic. That is,
however, not to say it is carefree, because it is not. And
neither do I mean to imply that difficult and unpleasant
things do not come our way, because they do. But the
goodness and satisfaction of our lifestyle is authentic. The
joy and peace in our family is real.

All of this originates with our Christian faith and rests
on the fundamental truth that God is in total control. He
orchestrates the circumstances of our life for His good
purposes. This is the very definition of His being sovereign.

Understanding and accepting God's absolute sovereignty
is foundational to living a godly life. Whenever I talk about
The Good Life, what I mean is a godly life lived within an
agrarian paradigm.

I do not believe you can remove godly living and still
realize The Good Life. You can have a lesser imitation but
not the genuine article. All of which leads me to the subject
of contentment, which is another vital part of The Good
Life.

To my way of thinking, contentment is the same as being
satisfied and comfortable with God's provision, with His
blessings. It is, very simply, the humble acceptance of His
sovereignty and will.

On the other hand, *dis*contentment is pride, it is anger, it
is war against God's providence. It is the same as saying to
Him: "This is not enough! I want more!" Discontentment
breeds bitterness and rebellion, and worse.

Instead of working and waiting patiently for God's greater provision (if He so chooses to grant it), the discontented person gets what he wants by other means: plunging into debt, questing for wealth, and even stealing, which, to my way of thinking, includes culturally acceptable forms of theft, like taking government grants or other handouts of taxpayer dollars.

Those who live with a proper understanding of their relationship to God understand that, because of Adam's sin, God doesn't owe us anything more than death and damnation. That this Holy Sovereign would send His sinless Son to live among us and then die a cruel death to atone for our sins is difficult to comprehend. This alone is far more than we deserve. That He then meets the basic needs of those who call Him Lord (and many who do not) is further evidence of His incredible goodness. That, in most instances, He grants us gifts far beyond our genuine needs is a further manifestation of His grace (getting what you *don't* deserve) and mercy (not getting what you *do* deserve).

Nevertheless, after all such blessings are embraced and enjoyed, God's people are prone to whine and cry and moan and complain. We have the audacity to believe we should have more. Some even think to themselves that they deserve more. This is nothing short of a crime, and when we do this sort of thing, we open ourselves up to very bad consequences.

The spirit of discontentment is always there, in the shadows, watching. He dogs you, waiting for his opportunity, waiting to exploit your weakness. He will let you first entertain those other spirits: jealousy, envy, covetousness, and materialism. They will lead you off the path. They will tear at your soul. They will weaken your faith. They will marinate you in their sourness. Finally, they will deliver you to the demon. And when discontentment sinks his teeth into you, the joy and peace of godly contentment leave.

It is sad to see discontent in others. It is sadder yet to see it in ourselves.

7

My Son
Bought an Axe

L AST YEAR, WHEN HE WAS TEN, MY YOUNGEST
son bought himself an axe. Not a little hatchet, but a
full-size axe. He bought it from the Western Auto
store on Main Street in Moravia for $15. It's a nice axe for
$15.

I did not know my son was going to buy an axe. I came
home from work one day, and Marlene informed me, "James
bought himself an axe today." Of course, he bought it with
his mother's permission. And, after 25 years of marriage,
Marlene knows me well enough to know that I would not
object. Fact is, she knew I would be downright pleased with
the purchase.

And I was truly pleased. Instead of a toy or a treat, my
son had, for the first time in his life, used his money (which
he does not have a lot of) to buy a tool. An agrarian tool, I
might add. Furthermore, this is no modern, self-powered
tool; it is a tool that requires considerable manual effort to
operate. And it requires a measure of skill, too. Indeed, I
was *very* pleased.

Some will cringe at the thought of a 10-year-old boy
running wild, wielding an axe. He might hurt himself. He
might hurt someone else. He might do property damage.
Well, yes, he might.

But this is not just any boy we are talking about. This is
my son, and I know my son's character. I know him to be
responsible. What's more, I have taught each of my sons
how to safely use an axe. This does not guarantee that they
will never hurt themselves. There are no guarantees when it
comes to such things.

That is where a father's prayers for God's protection over his family come into play. While a mother's prayers are as vital and important as are a father's prayers, I believe that a father's prayers are somehow different. A father has the God-ordained responsibility to lead, protect, and provide for his family, and prayer is an integral part of properly doing each of those things. Without a father's prayers, the family suffers. So I pray, and I trust God.

What, you may be wondering, does a 10-year-old need his own axe for? Well, for the same reason a grown man needs an axe. When James bought it, he put it right to use splitting small chunks of firewood.

He also uses it to hone his skills, chopping away at fallen trees lying in our woods. If it's dead and on the ground, it's fair game. If it's dead and standing, and bigger around than a man's wrist, it's off limits. Chopping a live tree is grounds for having one's axe taken away—or worse.

Then, of course, you can use your axe to lop a chicken's head off before you make a meal of it. James has not done that yet, but I'm sure he would be willing.

⁂

We can damage our young boys by overprotecting
them and by creating fear that they may get hurt.
Little boys who are constantly overprotected
are in jeopardy of having their masculinity
warped. Obviously we are to teach them to use
good judgement. But we are not to squelch their
aggressiveness. They will survive the scars and
broken bones of boyhood. But they cannot survive
being feminized through the perpetual fear of
getting hurt. God made boys to be aggressive.
—Steve Farrar
Point Man

8

Boys Working Together

WHO NEEDS A TRACTOR WHEN YOU HAVE A 1993 Ford Taurus station wagon and three sons? That is what I thought to myself today as I stood watching my boys working together to pull logs out of our woods.

Years ago, before I had children, I bought a tractor. It was an old Farmall C in very fine condition. I think I paid $700 for it. I bought that tractor even though Marlene and I were landless newlyweds, living in a two-room apartment in town. I really had no use for it. I bought it because it was beautiful, and a farmer I knew and trusted told me it was a good bargain.

The tractor ended up behind my father-in-law's house. Before long, I sold it. I was putting the cart before the horse. $700 was a lot of money to me then (still is!), and we were saving to buy land.

Well, we eventually bought some land, built a homestead, and we have managed without a tractor all this time. Which brings me to the car . . . .

The station wagon is a faded gray Ford Taurus that has been our family vehicle for the past ten years. It has 165,000 miles on it and has been a decent unit, but it has become a piece of junk. It started to enter the "junk" stage years ago when the engine literally dropped down onto the road at a busy city intersection. The car is replete with dents and scratches and rust. The upholstery has been ravaged from hauling boys and stuff. The engine rattles. And mice live in it.

When the mice move in, the end is near. It's a sure sign. They know.

I once had a pickup truck that was in much the same shape as our Taurus. I was driving down the road one day and a mouse climbed up onto the seat beside me. The little creature sat there looking at me. He was, I suspect, amazed that I was still driving the thing. The truck didn't last much longer.

As with an old and sick family pet there comes a day when you have to put your vehicle away. But, before that happens, many agrarians will put their cars and trucks "out to pasture" for awhile. That's what I did with the old Taurus. I parked it out of the way in the side yard earlier this spring.

Then came the decision to have a bonfire at the little hoe-down we're planning here for the 4th of July. I started hauling free-for-the-taking pallets home from the local lumber yard in preparation for the big event.

My boys came up with the idea of using the car to haul logs out of the woods for the bonfire. The logs are down an embankment behind our house, the remaining carcasses of once-tall trees that have died, fallen to the ground, and largely decayed. Some are quite big. I questioned whether a station wagon on its last legs had the *uumph!* to do the job, but what was there to lose? I agreed to the idea.

Sundry lengths of rope and chain and nylon strapping were rounded up to do the pulling. My oldest son, Chaz, backed the car up to the edge of the woods. A log was selected and secured. With the "check engine" light flashing red (it has done that for a couple years now), Chaz slowly pulled ahead. Knots and chain hooks slipped loose, but these setbacks were overcome.

Robert, my middle son, stayed with the log, helping to maneuver it around obstacles. James, my youngest, positioned himself halfway between, intercepting and relaying messages: "Go! Keep Going! Stop! . . . Stop! . . . STOP!!! Back Up! Okay, go again!"

That old automobile had a lot of get-up-and-go. In fact, it was surprisingly powerful. It wouldn't pull every log they wanted to get, but it pulled some big 'uns outta there.

Once a log was up onto the lawn, they backed the car up, shortened the long towline, and rehitched the log. Robert and James positioned themselves in the back, with the hatch up, while Chaz slowly towed the log out to the road and up to the end of our property. Then he reentered the lawn and pulled around to the selected bonfire location. When the log was unhitched, they all headed back for another.

Though their tools were not those of a professional logger, my sons were, nevertheless, logging. They were also being resourceful. What's more, they were learning to work together to do a big job. It was a very good thing.

Once again, the richness of rural living manifested itself. Do children who live in the suburban centers have these experiences? I lived in the suburbs as a boy, and I do not remember doing anything like this. My children have a better life than I did. Of this I am very certain.

I watched all of this unfold from the windows of my house. I was captivated by the wonder of three healthy boys, these sons that God has entrusted to me, working with such gusto and focus. They did not need my help. They had conceived and were executing this work on their own, and they were doing the job well. They were working like men.

Marlene saw me watching with the look of a well-pleased father and said to me, "Now there is something you can write about."

Work is not a curse;
it is the prerogative of intelligence,
the only means to manhood,
and the measure of civilization.
—Calvin Coolidge

In most of human history and over most of the world,
man has had no alternative to agriculture. Only in
recent times did it occur to us to abandon the
ancient norm and leave our food production in
the hands of a few specialists. The final cost of
this risky experiment has not been measured.
But it is clear that we are using and destroying more
resources than any generation in history. And it is
becoming more obvious that the food produced by mass
industrialized cultivation is inferior, unwholesome
and sometimes dangerous.
—Howard King

When I was a boy in the countryside . . .
people [gardened] for self-sufficiency, for it
would not have occurred to them to do otherwise.
People were self-reliant because they had to be; it
was a way of life. They were doing what
generations had done before them; simply carrying
on a traditional way of life. Money was a rare
commodity, far too valuable to be spent on things
you could grow or make yourself . . .
they would have laughed at a diet of store-bought foods.
—John Seymour
The Self Sufficient Gardener

9

Industrial Providers

(Understanding the Oligopoly)

F EW PEOPLE REALIZE THAT A SMALL GROUP OF huge, wealthy, and powerful global corporations controls the overwhelming majority of food production and distribution in the world today. Con-Agra, Cargill, and Archer Daniels Midland are among the biggest. These corporations are continually entering into partnerships and joint ventures with other huge global corporations like Monsanto, DuPont, and Philip Morris, to create profitable economic alliances.

The net result of these alliances has been the creation of an incredibly complex and ever-changing global food oligopoly. An oligopoly is an economic system in which the market is dominated by a small number of sellers. A *mono*poly, on the other hand, is an economic system which is control by one seller. There is, in the final analysis, not a whole lot of difference between the two.

The industrial food oligopoly is supranational; it transcends national boundaries, interests, and to a large degree, national authority. Furthermore, it has a single overriding purpose for existing: to make money in order to make its stockholders wealthy.

These mega-corporations have the financial resources to buy anything they want. Their money talks. It says, "Don't bite the hand that feeds you." Politicians are cheap. Grants to supposedly unbiased college research programs are more costly. But it is all just another business expense that serves to add more money to the bottom line.

With that bottom line always in mind, the oligopoly endeavors to own and/or control every aspect of food production, beginning with the genetically-modified and patented seed that must be purchased from it, on through the food system, culminating in packaged food on your grocery store shelf. To an astounding and alarming degree, these industrial providers have been very successful in their endeavors.

Within this modern system of food production, farmers are no longer the independent producers they once were. Instead, they are pressured to integrate into the industrial system, to join alliances where they become "growers." They provide labor and sometimes a bit of capital, but they are, for all practical purposes, servants to the global corporations. They must play by the industrial providers' rules or they are out of the game. Those rules are not made by people who understand and appreciate farmers; they are made by corporate strategists with soft hands and clean fingernails who are always, always looking at the bottom line.

The Leviathan corporations own laboratories, mills, grain storage facilities, broiler factories, hatcheries, feedlots, stockyards, meat-packing facilities, food-processing factories, fertilizer factories, pesticide factories, railroad cars, barges, trucks, and so on. They have close control over the "vertically integrated" food system that serves *their* best interests.

Global industrial control and manipulation of food and agriculture by the oligopoly has destroyed and continues to destroy the vitality of rural farming communities. Such areas are nothing more than mining outposts to the globalist masters.

Proportionately little of the monetary wealth that is derived from the land stays and circulates in the communities where it is produced, as was once the case. Now the wealth flows out of the mines and into the coffers of the oligopoly. It reinvests profits wherever it best suits the bottom line . . . Africa, Asia, South America . . . wherever there is cheap natural wealth and labor to exploit.

When an agricultural mining operation is no longer profitable, it is shut down and abandoned. The biblical concept of sustainable farming is anathema to the corporate profiteers. The idea of being good stewards of God's creation is a joke to them.

In the wake of its irresponsibilities, the oligopoly will "make it all better" with the slickest public relations campaigns that money can buy. Television commercials, glossy magazine placements, whatever it takes. When it is done with its marketing magic, gullible Moderns will believe that the industrial providers are the best friend a farmer and the environment ever had!

But they are liars. Industrialism has done more to destroy healthy farming communities, the productive power of the soil, and natural resources than any other destructive force on earth. Farm families, rural communities, and the environment take a back seat to the almighty dollar that the oligopoly worships. That, my friend, is the *real* bottom line!

God has never looked upon concentrations of human power and control favorably. Manifestations of greed and pride invite judgment. God alone is sovereign over His creation. He will not suffer the oligopoly to stand indefinitely. It will run its course and, in His time, fall apart because it is neither physically nor spiritually sustainable.

For those who have the eyes to see, the vulnerabilities of the industrial food system are clearly evident. Primary among these is the following reality:

The free flow of cheap food is entirely
connected to, and dependent on, the
free flow of cheap oil.

Cheap oil is history. Continued easy availability of oil at any price is threatened by four tenuous factors: terrorism, war, natural disasters, and economic breakdown. Each of these things has the potential to disrupt the free flow of oil. Each of these variables can and will, to some degree, negatively affect the hyper-refined division of labor and the just-in-time delivery system that the free flow of industrial food depends on.

The price of food will go much higher. You can count on it. Oil shortages and high energy costs must trickle down to the food consumers. Perhaps the trickle will turn to a flow. God only knows how things will play out.

One thing is certain: when the global food system fails to any significant degree, people will go hungry. Those who are unable to provide for themselves and their families could starve. I am not talking about this happening in some third world country. The industrial providers do not cater to and depend on third world countries. Their customers are those who live in developed nations of the world. People like you.

As I said when I began this story, few people understand how the global food system works. They do not realize how dependent they are on the oligopoly. And they really do not care. But they should. Someday they will. Unfortunately, by then, it might be too late to do them any good.

By the way, it was not all that long ago that America had a decentralized system of agriculture and food production. It worked very well. Decentralized agrarianism always does.

❧

We are going to have to gather up the
fragments of knowledge and responsibilities
that have been turned over to governments,
corporations, and specialists, and put
those fragments back together again
in our own minds and in our families
and households and neighborhoods.
—Wendell Berry
A Continuous Harmony: Essays Cultural & Agricultural

IO

Hay Help

THIS LAST MONDAY WAS HOT. SOMEONE SAID it got to over 100 degrees. The humidity was way up there, too. Health professionals on news reports were warning the Moderns to stay inside and not exert themselves. But the local farmers (what few are left) ignored all that and made hay. That's because hay can only be made when the sun shines. And the hotter it is, the better.

Monday was also the day my 14-year-old son, Robert, was asked if he wanted to help unload hay wagons for a nearby farmer. The opportunity came to him by way of my son's friend who works for the farmer when needed. Unloading hay wagons is something Robert had never done before, but he did not hesitate to say yes.

I learned about all this later in the day, after I returned home from my non-agrarian regular job. Marlene pulled into the driveway and Robert bounded from the car into my workshop to tell me what he had done. He was excited. He was practically glowing.

He told me of the hay wagons, jumbled full of bales. He told me how he pulled them free and handed them off to his friend, who, standing in the doorway, dropped each one onto the inclined "elevator" that conveyed the bales up into the haymow. People at the other end neatly stacked the bales.

He used one hay hook and one free hand to do the work. He and his friend unloaded four wagons. He showed me the dirt on his body that came from the chaff that landed on sweat and stuck. He told me his neck itched. He showed me his forearms, scratched from the hard stubble in the densely packed bales. He told me he drank lots of cold water from a hose in the milk house, then he he helped feed some calves.

I am not being melodramatic when I tell you that a wave of emotion swept over me as I heard my son recount what he had done that day. He had experienced a wonderful rural rite-of-passage that so few boys nowadays will ever know. But more, much more, than merely experiencing it, he loved it.

My mind drifted back to when I was two years older than my son is now. I was a refugee from suburbia. My parents bought a house here in the rolling green hills of the Finger Lakes region of upstate New York. It is farm country. It is dairy and corn and hay country. It is God's country.

Before long, I started working for local farmers, helping to bring in the hay. Such work is always hard but it is especially so when you are new to it. The hooks in your hands are awkward, as are the heavy bales. The seasoned veterans working with you plod along, making it all look so easy, while you struggle. It can be quite comical, though you do not think so at the time. Eventually, if you stick with it, you get more comfortable, confident, strong, and even a bit cocky.

I stuck with it. Through my teens and into my early 20s, I handled a lot of hay (and straw). I have good memories of those days. The choicest of those memories are the times when, after a long hot afternoon of unloading wagons, dark storm clouds loomed in the western sky. There were full wagons yet to unload. Time was short. Urgency set in, and the race was on. I liked to be in the wagon at times like that.

The man unloading the wagon sets the pace. The normal pace was three or four bales, spaced out along the length of the elevator. The distance between the bales would be equivalent to two or three bales. But Urgency called for more. My challenge was to send them up with no spaces between the bales. For those in the mow, the challenge was to deal with it. This is when testosterone and determination kick in. The adrenaline will shortly follow . . . .

With a hay hook in each hand, my pace picks up, my focus narrows. Sweat is running from every pore of my body. I feel my heart pounding hard and steady in my chest, and the pressure of each pulse is in my ears. I am reaching, hooking, pulling, bale after bale, in quick succession. A cloud of chaff floats in the air, collecting into a thin green poultice on my forearms. My hooks, polished bright by untold thousands of blades of dry grass, flash in the glorious golden rays that bathe the land before a summer storm hammers you with its fury.

I am reaching, hooking, pulling, turning, dropping the bales, one after another, with perfect precision into the channel of the inclined elevator. There is no hesitation in my movements, no wasted motions. It is an agrarian ballet, being worked with the intensity of a madman. Reaching, hooking, pulling, now two at a time, to the doorway and into the elevator.

With the strained grimace and brute skill of an ancient warrior-champion on the battlefield, I do not parry with the enemy. There is no time. I sink my hooks and deftly dispatch each foe. I am a man with a mission. I am unstoppable. I am unbeatable.

First comes the cold wind, whipping the dry chaff on the ground near the barn into little cyclones. Then comes the rain; huge, hard, welcome, icy drops slam onto my hot skin as I throw the last cube of hay from the wagon. Then I stop, standing, watching that last bale make its way into the mow. And I think to myself how good it feels to have worked like a man.

I have never in my life felt more alive and strong and whole than I did back then, when I worked hard in the hot sun, unloading hay wagons and packing bales into the haymow. My son had a very small taste of this feeling on Monday. He wants more. I am pleased, and I am very thankful.

Before the rise of modern industry . . .
virtually the whole of humankind lived in
family-centered economies. The family was
the locus of the most productive activity,
whether it be on largely self-sufficient farms
or in small family shops. . . Husbands and wives
relied on each other, needed each other,
shared with each other, so their small family
enterprises might succeed. They specialized
in their daily tasks, according to their
respective skills. Marriage was still true
to its historic definition: a union of the
sexual and the economic.
—Allan C. Carlson, Ph.D.
Love is Not Enough:
Toward The Recovery of a Family Economics

And we must be careful to see that the old
cultural centers of home and community were
made vulnerable to this invasion [of industrialism]
by their failure as economies. If there is no
household or community economy, then family
members and neighbors are no longer useful to
one another. When people are no longer useful to
one another, then the centripetal force of family
and community fails, and people fall into depen-
dence on exterior economies and organizations.
—Wendell Berry
What Are People For?

44

II

Returning to the Family Economy

W E LIVE IN AN INDUSTRIAL ECONOMY. SOME say we are actually now in a service economy. If so, it is still a part of the industrial paradigm. In such an economy, the typical family is not a producer of goods. It is a collection of individual consumers. This is the way the industrial providers like it to be. They want everyone to be dependent on them. But that is contrary to the historical pattern. For hundreds of years prior to the industrial revolution, families were self-reliant, integrated units of efficient production. This historical model of family-based production is referred to by historians and economists as the *family economy*.

In a properly functioning family economy, every member of the family—father, mother, children, grandparents, and any extended family living under the same roof—plays a role in making the family as self-sufficient as possible. Everyone works for the good of the family. Everyone is needed.

This model is naturally suited to farming and homesteading. It was the norm in agrarian America prior to the mid-1800s. Many farm families tenaciously held on to some form of this lifestyle well into the 20th century. Today it is an anachronism, but that may be changing.

The family economy has, in times past, also included numerous cottage industries. Grain milling, candlemaking, tinsmithing, blacksmithing, coopering, carriage-making, and furniture-making are just a few examples of small-scale home businesses that contributed to the economy of many families. Each of these crafts and services was performed in, or just outside, the home. Such homes would also have gardens and some livestock. Even in the villages, it was not unusual to have a family milk cow. Again, self-sufficiency and thus, survival of the family, was the collaborative objective.

Within the family economy, mothers and fathers taught their children the many different skills associated with their way of life. The whole idea was to train children to be productive members of the family as children so they would become productive, self-reliant leaders (and teachers) of their own families one day. The virtues of thrift, hard work, family closeness, and religious faith, were integral elements of these families of yore and produced men and women of great character.

The primary objective of the family economy was not to make a lot of money. It was to sustain a way of life. Indeed, most farming was subsistence farming, which means the family produced just about everything they needed, bartered for what they did not have, and did not require a lot of money.

That kind of life is hard for us to imagine these days. We figure subsistence farmers must have been poor miserable beings, barely surviving. But these were people who knew how to make the land produce and, for the most part, they operated thriving farms and homesteads. They had what they needed to live a good and full life.

It is my strongly-held belief that in order to build strong families and reestablish a vibrant agrarian culture, individual families must rediscover and deliberately work towards reuniting the entire family into some sort of family economy.

Most agrarians clearly see that the blending of family life and work into a more self-sufficient family economy is the ideal. It is something they dream of and work towards. I am one of those people.

But the reality of the situation is, unless you are born into an already-established family business or you are independently wealthy, a true and complete family economy is not easily accomplished in this modern world.

Those families living prior to the mid-1800s did not have exorbitant property taxes extorted from them to pay for government schooling schemes. There was no federal income tax to support a bloated and oppressive federal bureaucracy. Spending on social programs was minimal. Life, health, auto, property, and unemployment insurances were, I'm guessing, not even around (certainly not auto).

Money was the real thing—gold and silver, not the fiat currency that governments so conveniently devalue through inflation. Huge stores full of manufactured goods, which we've been conditioned to think we must have, were not around back then either. Children were not being bombarded with messages to continually be buying the latest whatever.

For new agrarians in the 21st century to reestablish family economies, we need to, first, get out of bondage to debt. A key part of doing this is to simplify our needs and wants; we must tame our tendency toward materialism and consumerism. Then we must endeavor to supply as many of our family's needs as possible. And finally, we must also create family businesses that generate enough actual money to pay the most necessary of living costs in our very expensive industrial economy.

All of this is an enormous challenge. It is not something that most people can do overnight. But it is something that most people can begin on a small scale and slowly, deliberately, bring to fruition.

There are some brave and innovative pioneers who are establishing wonderful examples of godly family economies. Joel Salatin* comes to mind immediately. There are many others testing the waters and paving the way. If the task were easy, more people would be doing it. Nevertheless, the goal of bringing fathers home and reuniting families in life and work is noble and necessary. The difficulty of attaining an ideal is no excuse for not pursuing it.

---

* Joel Salatin operates Polyface Farm in Swoope, Virginia. He is one of America's foremost advocates for sustainable farming. To date, Joel has authored five books that teach others how to follow his example. I think his best book is *Family Friendly Farming: A Multigenerational Home-Based Business Testament*.

The pre-industrial family bears little resemblance
to the family of today. Partly as a result of the
destruction of the village, partly as a result of
laws designed to weaken family bonds, and
partly because of economic pressure that forced
members of families to become independent and
mobile units of labor, partly because of the rise
of individualism and egalitarian ideologies, and
partly because of the intrusion of the cult of
efficiency into every area of life, the family has
become a mere shadow of its former self. As a
result, the family became inefficient at the tasks
it used to do so well. Other institutions rose to
take over these functions, and the home became
a place to eat and sleep—no longer a place to
work—no longer a place to live.
—Howard King
A Christian Critique of Technological Society

Nor is love enough to hold a family
together . . . Meaningful family survival
depends on the building and maintenance of a
true household economy, one that exists apart
from the national and international economies . . .
Toward [this end], both men and women are
still called home to relearn and recommit to
the deeper meanings of the ancient words
husbandry and housewifery.
—Allan C. Carlson, Ph. D.
From Cottage to Work Station

12

A Summer Evening's Meal

F EW THINGS IN LIFE ARE MORE PLEASING TO
the sensibilities of agrarians than to eat food they
have grown, harvested, and prepared with their own
hands, preferably on their own land. Game and other wild
victuals gleaned from the surrounding woods, fields, and
streams surely qualifies too. This act of providing one's own
food is an acknowledgment and acceptance of the Divine
order. It is an expression of obedience. It is the realization of
freedom.

There have been times when my family sat down to a
meal that came entirely from the cornucopia of our own
little homestead. Such wholesome feasts are truly special
because they represent something we value and aspire to do
even more.

The next best thing, and almost as satisfying, is to sit
down to a meal in which each victual is locally grown, by
real people, people you actually know by name. As a matter
of fact, my family did this very thing last evening.

Yesterday was a Thursday in July. That means it was
farmers' market day in Skaneateles, New York, a town one-
half hour from our home in the Finger Lakes region. Most
every Thursday during the market season, my lovely wife,
Marlene, is there, under a white tent, selling her home-baked
breads. As usual, she came home from the market yesterday
with the bread all sold and a selection of fresh produce
from the other vendors.

Marlene bought some perfectly-ripened, hoop-house-
grown tomatoes from the Hewitt family. The Hewitts are
Mennonites, and this is the second year they have grown

early tomatoes for the market. My own garden tomatoes are doing well but are still green and probably a couple weeks from being ready.

With Brendan and Michelle, who grow produce at Tierra Farm, Marlene traded a loaf of her "Nutty-Grain" bread for new potatoes and little turnips. I am not growing either of those vegetables this year.

Marlene traded a loaf of "Oatmeal-Raisin" bread to Rose Ryan, another organic farmer, for some beets and fennel. My beets are still small and I have never considered growing fennel, but maybe I should, because my kids love it. They chew the stalks like celery. Rose also grows German Red Stiffneck garlic and has won awards for her decorative garlic braids.

From Bob Harsford, Marlene bought sweet corn and cucumbers. This corn is the first of the season for us, and I don't know how Bob has managed to have it ready so early. I have a small bed of corn in my garden this year but it is not sweet corn. I decided to try growing some popcorn. As for cucumbers, I have four varieties planted, but I got them in a little late.

By the way, Marlene could not remember Bob's name when she saw him again at the market this year. He told her it is easier to remember it backwards: boB. Now she will never forget.

Heather is the young woman who sells beautiful bouquets of flowers at the market. She gave Marlene two of her bouquets in appreciation for the help that Marlene and our boys gave her when setting up and taking down her tent. I can tell you my wife is enjoying those flowers more than she is vegetables!

Our evening meal revolved around all these fresh goods from the market. Marlene and I sat down with the boys to eat at the picnic table in our back yard. It was a beautiful time of day. The oppressively hot sun was dropping, the air was cooling nicely, and a balmy breeze was discernible. I asked the blessing, thanking God for His provision. I specifically thanked Him for each kind of food on the table before us.

We had the tomatoes and cucumbers chopped up with some oil and vinegar dressing. The little potatoes from Tierra Farm were nicely boiled, with their thin red skins still in place. boB's sweet corn was sweet and good. I ate mine without butter or salt, as I always do. We had grilled hamburgers too. The meat came from a cow raised by our all-the-way-back-to-high school friends, Ken and Mary Pearsall. The slices of bread on either side of the burgers were Marlene's "Cracked Wheat & Oat." Ice water was just fine to wash it all down.

It was a simple meal. It was a good meal. It was the kind of meal that I love to eat with my family on a summer evening. It was nothing special but it was everything special, if you know what I mean.

❦

The family dinner table represents the connection we have with each other. Each person sitting at the table isn't there by accident, but is a God-given gift and a specific fit for your family. If I had the opportunity to give every woman on the planet a gift, it would be a vase of flowers for the middle of their dinner tables to remind them that this is a sacred place where their families are not only fed but are nurtured and loved—where heartstrings are tied and relationships realigned.
—Leanne Ely

*Good bread is the most fundamentally
satisfying of all foods; and good bread
with fresh butter, the greatest of feasts.*
—James Beard

⁂

*A crust eaten in peace
is better than a banquet
partaken in anxiety.*
—Aesop

⁂

*How can a nation be great
if its bread tastes like Kleenex?*
—Julia Child

⁂

*Dry bread at home
is better than roast meat abroad.*
—George Herbert

⁂

*I understand the big food companies
are developing a tearless onion.
I think they can do it—after all,
they've already given us tasteless bread.*
—Robert Orben

13

A Small Example
of Family Economy

I N THE PREVIOUS STORY I MENTIONED THAT MY
wife, Marlene, bakes bread and sells it in Skaneateles,
New York on Thursday afternoons through the summer
months. Marlene has sold in three different farmer's markets
over the past five years and Skaneateles has, by far, been
the best. She knows the discouragement of baking many
hours then sitting at the market several more hours, and
returning home with most of her goods unsold because so
few people showed up. This does not happen in
Skaneateles.

Now my dear wife exhausts herself with hours of baking,
goes to the market, and comes home refreshed and renewed
by the people who come to her table, week after week, pur-
chasing almost everything she makes and giving her praise
and encouragement for the down-home goodness of her
products. They also give her $3.75 for a loaf of bread which
I think is well worth $5.00.

Marlene does the market for the money, but the money is
really of secondary importance. More importantly, she
participates in the market because it is a satisfying creative
outlet and an excellent learning experience for our
sons—they can make money and learn some valuable
lessons in the process. And maybe, just maybe, Marlene is
laying the foundation for a much more significant family
economy.

In the first years of my wife's little bread business, my
oldest son, Chaz, benefitted most. He was very involved in
helping to make, package, and sell the bread at market. This
was, essentially, his summer job, and it provided him with a
few hundred dollars of income over the season.

This year, Chaz has a summer job at the lumber yard in Moravia, so the other two boys (who participated in smaller ways in the market before) have stepped up to the plate. Robert, my 14-year-old, makes many small loaves of zucchini bread. My 10-year-old son, James, makes cookies.

Under Marlene's tutelage, these boys make their bread and cookies on Wednesday and help Marlene as needed on Thursday. They load the SUV, go to market, set up the tent and tables, and actively participate in selling the goods. When the flow of customers tapers off near the end of the market, the boys often entertain themselves for awhile at a nearby playground. They'll return to help pack everything away when it's time to go home.

My sons enjoy doing this with their mother because it is fun, and their baked goods typically sell out, which means they end up making money. Robert usually clears $40 to $50, and James $15 to $20.

My boys are gaining tremendously useful life skills as they interact with customers, make change, visit with other vendors, and soak up the "agri-preneurial" culture of the market. What's really nice is that the children of some other vendors are also there helping their parents and learning all these good things, too.

My sons have occasionally marketed some vegetables from our home garden, and they've sold well. It makes me think that I should plant a small market garden on my neighbor's property, since I have no more room and he has very kindly given me permission. I may have the kids help me grow a few particular vegetables that they can sell, and after repaying me for the seed, they can have the money. This is a way to expand the family economy we already have, and for me to become more involved. Of course, I'll have to give up something I'm already doing to make the time for this.

It has occurred to me that a home bakery with a weekly home-delivery bread route would be a perfect foundation to build that more significant home economy I mentioned earlier. Pleased bread customers would, I'm certain, be purchasers of eggs, meat, fruits, vegetables, and crafts produced by our family.

I see a lot of opportunity. But it requires more land, and I will not go into debt to finance my dreams. I will wait on the Lord to provide as He sees fit, in His time. Until then, we will bloom where we are planted.

The small family economy that Marlene has built around the farm market has been, and continues to be, a very good thing. I'm thankful for this wonderful experience my sons are getting. And I'm also very thankful for the industrious wife with whom God has blessed me.

❧

The best things in life are nearest:
Breath in your nostrils, light in your eyes,
flowers at your feet, duties at your hand,
the path of right just before you.
Then do not grasp at the stars,
but do life's plain, common work as it comes,
certain that daily duties and daily bread
are the sweetest things in life.
—Robert Louis Stevenson

A happy family
is an earlier heaven.
—John Bowring

❧

When you look at your life,
the greatest happinesses
are family happinesses.
—Joyce Brothers

❧

The life of the nation
is the life of the family written large.
—Plato

❧

The happiest moments of my life
have been the few which I have
passed at home in the bosom of my family.
—Thomas Jefferson

❧

There is no doubt that it is
around the family and the home
that all the greatest virtues,
the most dominating virtues of
human society, are created,
strengthened and maintained.
—Winston Chruchill

14

The Phone Call

I PICKED UP MY HOME PHONE LAST THURSDAY night to hear the dial tone giving an intermittent signal. That's what it does when I have a voicemail message. I dialed the phone company and punched in my "secret" code number:

> Hello, this is Alice Conwell. I was at the farmer's market today and purchased some molasses cookies from your son.

This is where my heartbeat started to pick up. I listened intently and braced myself for bad news. Had something gone wrong? Did someone get sick from one of James's cookies? Had an errant Lego gotten in the batter and broken a tooth?

> I grew up eating molasses cookies my whole life and I have never had any so absolutely delicious as those.

Wow, what a relief! I relaxed, yelled to James that he had a message, and kept listening.

> I ate four in a row and went for a fifth. I just cannot believe how absolutely fabulous they were. And I notice on the ingredients that you used olive oil in them, which I have never heard of. I just had to call and tell your son that I am a cookie eater, I have eaten cookies all over the world, and these are

some of the *best* cookies I have *ever* eaten in my entire life. So I just had to let him know. They were worth every single cent I paid for them, and he just made my entire evening. So have a nice day and I'll see you next week at the market.

I handed the phone to James and hit the button to replay the message. He listened seriously. A few moments later, a big smile spread across his face.

"Alice Conwell" is a fictitious name I've given the actual young woman who called. She comes to the Skaneateles Farmer's Market each week with her four small children. I am thankful for her phone call (which I have transcribed here word for word). It was so nice, and it meant a lot to my 10-year-old cookie-making son.

I believe all children need to have a special skill or a special interest that is theirs alone. It is something they derive self-worth and satisfaction from. It is something that helps shape their identity. For boys, this thing could be hunting, it could be raising a particular kind of animal, it could be restoring tractors, trapping, woodworking, small engine repair, or any number of other things. Whatever it is, it's their thing.

My son, James, has several interests. One of them is making cookies and selling them at the farmer's market. He owns this niche in our little family economy. Now, one of his very pleased customers has acknowledged his skill and ability. Her sincere positive reinforcement of his special skill has encouraged his entrepreneurial efforts. He wants to make more and different kinds of cookies to sell. This is a very good thing.

15

Dag Hammarskjold School #6

TODAY WHILE WORKING MY NON-AGRARIAN regular job, I had to journey into the inner city of Rochester, New York, two hours from my home. I do not go to big cities often and when I do, it is usually only because I must.

I found myself driving through neighborhoods where the cultures manifested themselves most visibly through the many businesses, myriad marketing messages, and the way the people dressed. They were foreign cultures to me. The place was, and the people were, the antithesis of everything agrarian. I thought to myself that I should lock my doors, just to be on the safe side.

My destination was Dag Hammarskjold School #6, which is currently closed for summer recess. Once there, I found myself walking down the halls of this multistory building, peering into the open doorways of empty classrooms, each just like the others.

I was struck by the realization that this was a dull, squalid, stifling place. And it further occurred to me that School #6 not only looked like an industrial factory, it was, for all practical purposes, exactly that.

Here was the place where "ministers" of the "benevolent" government bureaucracy worked tirelessly, day after day, year after year, to bend and shape the minds and souls of the children who are given over to them by the parents of this foreign culture. And here these children will be systematically institutionalized into the industrial paradigm.

No one else around me seemed cognizant of these things, nor concerned. I made an offhand comment about the factory-like atmosphere and no one responded. No one heard. I felt as if I were a character in a Ray Bradbury science fiction story or, perhaps, an episode of *The Twilight Zone*. It was spooky.

Before long, I left Dag Hammarskjold School #6. I shook the dust of that place off my feet and drove back to freedom, back to the quiet of my little homestead nestled on a green hillside in the Owasco Valley.

It had been a day of contrasts: urban culture versus agrarian culture; noise and busyness versus peace and quiet; blacktop versus fields; depravity versus fulfillment; confusion versus clarity; rebellion versus obedience; pride versus humility; curses versus blessings.

It was good to be home.

✀

The ancient walled city of the Bible had the most in common with the modern city. It was most often a center of apostasy, a base for imperialism, a treasure trove for plundering tyrants, a monument to human pride, vainglory and rebellion against God . . . The city provides no ideal for culture since it is opposed to biblical culture. Like Babel, the prototype, it has been erected in defiance of God's design for a decentralized agrarian civilization.
—Howard King
A Christian-Agrarian Critique of Technological Society

16

Raising Chickens
For Meat

FOR EIGHT YEARS IN A ROW, MY FAMILY HAS
raised chickens for meat. We do this for our own use,
not as a business. We raise anywhere from 50 to 75
Cornish chickens in a single batch each year. Cornish birds
are bred to grow fast and be extra meaty.

We order our chicks from a hatchery, and they are ship-
ped to us in a box through the mail. The post office in
Moravia calls the morning they show up and we go right
down to get them.

The chicks are loudly-chirping, golden-yellow puffballs
of activity. They are really cute. Eight to ten weeks later
they are not so cute, but they will be nicely fattened. They
dress out at four to four-and-a-half pounds each. A few
will be bigger, and a few will be smaller.

I keep new chicks inside my workshop, under a heat
lamp for a couple of weeks. Then we move them outside
into their pens. Fresh air, sunlight, and pasture are absolutely necessary to raise healthy, wholesome-to-eat birds.
Since I have such little land to work with, I let the lawn in
front of my house grow long, and that suffices for pasture.

My lawn is actually a former alfalfa field. It contains lots
of clover and weeds, along with some regular grass. I don't
fuss over it. I don't roll it in the spring or spray it with
anything to make it look better. I just try my best to keep it
mowed when chickens are not living there. As long as it is
green, I think my lawn looks just fine.

The chicken pens have sides and a top but no bottom;
they rest directly on the ground, allowing the birds full
access to the grass. This style of pen is often referred to as a
"chicken tractor." The tractors are moved by hand each day
to fresh patches of lawn.

When the birds get older and bigger they produce copious amounts of manure. That, and the overgrown grass, has a way of making my front yard look kind of disgraceful. But that's the price we pay for our own homegrown poultry with limited land. After a couple weeks, and a couple rains, and a couple mowings, the lawn once again looks acceptable.

Raising chickens like this on the front lawn is something that folks in towns and suburban neighborhoods would not appreciate or tolerate. I'm sure there are laws against it. I could probably be sent to jail for attempting to feed my family in this manner. But nobody around me complains. That's because there is nobody around me; they live up and down the road aways. I like my neighbors, but I like my privacy, too.

I have noticed that some people drive slowly by, very slowly, and crane their necks to see the spectacle of chicken tractors full of birds in my front yard. Some turn around at the end of the road and drive by again. I wonder what they are thinking?

I truly enjoy raising chickens for meat. I like to get up in the early morning, a little after 5:00, and go right outside to do my "chores" before heading off to do the less fulfilling work of my regular job.

I make sure the birds are moved to fresh grass, and that they have plenty of clean water and lots of high-protein feed, as the grass is only a small part of their diet. I tend to them again when I get home in the afternoon, and once more before dark. My boys help me as needed, but caring for the meat birds is mostly my job.

The entire family enjoys watching the chickens grow and interact with each other. We often sit on the ungrazed portion of the lawn by the tractor to watch the show. It's far better than television!

After gardening and keeping some hens for their eggs, raising chickens for meat is a logical next step towards greater food self-sufficiency. As my example proves, you don't need a whole lot of land to do it.

I sure enjoy raising chickens for meat. But I have to admit that I really do not like "harvesting" the crop. That's what I'll tell you about in my next story.

17

Pulling
Chicken Heads Off

WARNING: This story contains graphic descriptions that may appall and offend some non-agrarian readers.

I N THE PREVIOUS STORY, I TOLD HOW, FOR THE past eight years, my family has raised chickens for meat in our front yard, and how I enjoy being a small-scale chicken "farmer." Now I'd like to share a little about how we process our fatted fowls.

"Processing" is the current euphemism for what used to be known as "butchering" or, worse yet, "slaughtering." I have to admit that, no matter how much nicer it may sound, I do not enjoy processing chickens. Fact is, I find it downright disgusting. I can think of a whole lot of other things I would rather do.

Nevertheless, each year I harvest my flock of birds. I do this because a man's gotta do what a man's gotta do. For centuries, we men have killed, gutted, and cut up animals to feed ourselves and our families. There is no reason why I should not do this, and one big reason why I should. Namely, I must butcher my own birds in order to achieve greater self-sufficiency. It is part of being a Deliberate Agrarian.

I also must teach my sons this craft. Just because I grew up being a squeamish, sissified suburban boy doesn't mean they should, too.

Two of my sons are willing helpers on processing day. This pleases me greatly. My 17-year-old, however, wants nothing to do with butchering poultry. He has never had much interest in it. This saddens me but I remember feeling the same way at his age.

I want all my sons to embrace every manly agrarian skill they possibly can. I want them to know how to provide food for their families without needing it done for them by unknown specialists in some massive industrialized meat processing factory. I want this because I know that those who depend on the industrial providers are in bondage to those providers.

It is liberating to know you can butcher a chicken or, for that matter, any other kind of animal (and if you can do a chicken, you can do any other kind of animal). It is especially satisfying if you can do it skillfully. I am very serious when I tell you this.

To skillfully process a chicken, you must first process a great many of them. I have seen a video of Joel Salatin, the famous Virginia pasture poultry farmer, processing chickens. He is very fast and efficient, a true master of the craft. He is so fast, in fact, that the movie has to be slowed down to see exactly what he is doing. Joel became a master by butchering many thousands of chickens over the years.

I, on the other hand, have processed less than one thousand chickens. I am not a master. But I'm far, far better at it now than I was eight years ago. Every time I process a chicken I get more confident, and quicker, and better. When I have done my first thousand, I think I will be good at it.

Processing is done in our back yard. We set up a tent for shade. Over a couple of sawhorses we lay an old, 6-ft.-long, hernia-heavy, cast iron, double-bowl sink with drainboards on each side. The sink sat outside a barn for years, free for the taking. I hook a garden hose to the faucet for running water.

Chickens butcher best if you follow a logical and time-honored sequence of steps. First, the bird must be killed and the blood drained out. Then you dunk it up and down in hot water. This dunking is referred to as scalding and it loosens the feathers. Then you pick the feathers off. Then you remove the head, neck, and insides. That's all there is to it.

These steps will render a whole chicken, ready for the freezer. Or you can cut it up any way you like and freeze the parts. You can also can chicken. I have seen entire butchered

Banty hens stuffed into quart jars and canned that way. I would never have believed a whole chicken would fit in a canning jar until I saw it with my own eyes.

Killing

I end the life of my chickens in "killing cones," just as Joel Salatin does. The cones hold and restrain the birds. I suspend two cones over a wheelbarrow of sawdust, then gently upend the live birds into the cones. Their feet stick out the wide top of the cone, and their heads stick out the narrow bottom.

Then I hold the chicken's head with one hand and slice into the side of its neck with a sharp knife. After many messy and too-deep cuts, I have figured out where I need to slice in order to cut the artery on either side of the neck, without severing the windpipe.

The birds do not die immediately. They just look you in the eye while their hearts pump the blood out of their bodies. Then they die.

When I first ended the life of a chicken, it was not easy. I felt very bad about it. Now, after having done it so many times, I don't feel anything. The sissified suburban boy has grown up to become a cold-hearted, agrarian chicken killer.

Scalding

For many years I heated scalding water to 145-degrees in a big aluminium pot over a propane burner. I would hand-dunk the birds in the pot. It is a method that works very well. But proper water temperature is very important when it comes to getting the feathers off the birds, and maintaining a steady water temperature requires lighting and re-lighting the burner to carefully regulate the heat. That being the case, two years ago I developed my own gas-fired automatic chicken scalder.*

My new scalder is made from a water heater. Electronic controls automatically maintain the water temperature within a four-degree range. The scalder has a framework suspended over the water. I clip the feet of dead chickens onto the framework, with their heads aiming down, and flip a switch. A motor moves the critters into and out of the water at the rate of six dunks per minute. After a minute or so, I shut the dunker off and unclip the chickens. They are steaming hot and ready to pluck.

Plucking

Back in 1998 we handplucked our first chickens. It was not a pleasant thing. That experience motivated me to build my own automatic feather-plucking machine.* Now I simply drop the scalded birds in a tub, flip a switch, and watch as dozens of rubber plucker fingers flail the feathers off.

My homemade plucker will denude one to four chickens at a time. In about fifteen seconds, practically every feather is gone. It's hard to imagine how this could be true, but it is. I would not be processing my own birds if it was not for my automatic plucker.

Incidentally, my 10-and 14-year-old sons have become very adept at killing, scalding, and plucking. This is a tremendous help come processing day.

Head Removing

After the chicken is plucked, its head must be removed. Joel Salatin does not cut the bird's head off when he butchers. He says it takes too much time. So he pulls the head off . . . with his hands. Well, if that's the way Joel does it, that's the way I'll do it too!

You need physical strength and intestinal fortitude to pull a chicken's head off its neck. But, like anything else, with a little practice you get good at it. All my boys have pulled off chicken heads and *Marlene* has even done it a few times.

The first time my sweet wife pulled a chicken's head off was kind of funny. That she even decided to give it a try shocked me. With one hand holding the carcass of the bird on the

---

* Complete plans for building your own chicken plucker and scalder can be found in my books, *Anyone Can Build A Tub-Style Mechanical Chicken Plucker* and *Anyone Can Build A Whizbang Chicken Scalder*. For more information about these resources, see page 134.

sink drainboard, and her other hand around the critter's head, she pulled as hard as she could. The bird's neck was stretched right out but the head wouldn't come off. So we guys started yelling encouragement:

"Come on, Mom! You can do it! Pull! Pull harder! Harder! PULLLLLLLL!"

Marlene hung on to that chicken head, pulling with everything she had. It finally broke free. We all clapped and cheered like she was an Olympian who had just taken the gold. My children will long remember and cherish that special family moment. I'm sure they will tell their children of it.

Gutting

Once the head is removed, it's time to take the guts out. This is more politely known as eviscerating. I used to eviscerate by hand, but that was a hassle, so I recently made a little machine that does the job for me. Now I just stuff the headless bird inside the machine, flip a switch, and a few seconds later it pops out the other end, minus its insides. No mess, no fuss . . . .

Don't I wish! In reality, it takes a sharp knife and two bare hands to gut a chicken. Real men do not wear rubber gloves!

This is where I feel I should stop describing the process of processing a chicken. From here on out, it will take a whole lot of words, and unless you're really familiar with chicken anatomy, it won't make a lot of sense. Besides, it's not nearly as exciting as all the other stuff I've told you about.

Suffice it to say, you must cut the bird open at the back end, reach (with your bare hand) into the warm, slippery, slimy interior of the fowl, and pull everything in there out. Most of the "viscera" comes out very well. Some internal organs, however, do not want to let go. But they eventually will as you work at it. It is this gutting part that I dislike the most.

Everything I've told you about how to process a chicken is fresh in my mind because I took last Friday off from my regular job to harvest this year's flock of meat birds.

Marlene was busy making bread for a special weekend order. Robert, my 12-year-old, was not available, and my 17-year-old was conveniently working at his summer job. So it was me and James, my 10-year-old. He killed and scalded like a pro. I plucked and gutted.

There were numerous interruptions throughout the morning. After thirteen birds, we were sick of processing and took a break. In the afternoon, Marlene and Robert were able to help. Many hands make chicken processing go a whole lot easier and faster. We managed to get a total of 37 birds done that day.

The next day, we all went at it with renewed enthusiasm and knocked out the last 14 chickens in record time.

The crop is in our freezer now. Some birds are whole. Some are in parts; there are bags of wings, bags of legs, and bags of breasts. These will supply our chicken needs until next year's crop is harvested.

We also filled a couple big stock pots with necks, backs, and one tough old rooster that had been terrorizing our little flock of egglayers. Marlene added water and some vegetables and simmered the pots for a few hours. Then she strained off the liquid and canned it in quart jars. It isn't much to look at, but those jars of stock will be the base for many delicious homemade soups this winter.

It is a lot of work, but fun, to raise chickens. It is a lot of work, and not much fun, to process them. But it is all worthwhile when the work is done and the larder is full.

∞

Q: Why did the chicken cross the road?
A: Because a Deliberate Agrarian was after it.

18

Woodchuck Hunters

I AM ALMOST EMBARASSED TO TELL YOU THAT I was 18 years old before I shot a real gun. My sons did not have to wait so long. I taught my oldest son, Chaz, who is now 17, how to shoot when he was six. My other two boys learned just as early. I think it's important that boys learn gun safety and shooting skills when they are young. This could even be considered among the most important of agrarian skills.

Robert, my 14-year-old, and James, my 10-year-old, want to hunt. They want to hunt deer, turkey, squirrel, rabbit, and just about anything else that men hunt. After a trip to Maine, where we visited a moose weigh-in station on the first day of hunting season, they now dream of hunting moose. Much of their interest in this sort of thing comes from the Sugar Creek Gang* stories they listen to. Some of it comes from friends who hunt. These days they are hunting woodchucks.

Woodchucks are like pudgy vegetarian rats with short, furry tails and snub noses. They eat farm crops and burrow into fields, making holes and mounds of dirt. Sometimes

---

* Back in 1939, evangelist Paul Hutchens began writing a series of 36 Christian adventure stories. Each story revolves around the exploits of a rural group of boys who call themselves The Sugar Creek Gang. In recent years, all of these books have been dramatically read and recorded. The taped stories are exciting, wholesome, and God-honoring. My boys have listened to all 72 hours of the recordings . . . *many* times! You can purchase the tapes (or CDs) from Beloved Books, P.O. Box 878, Fenton, MI 48430. Phone: 810-735-0977. Internet: www.belovedbooks.com

farm equipment breaks because of the holes and mounds that woodchucks make. Farmers around here are glad to have someone shoot the woodchucks on their land.

My sons are well acquainted with *Marmota monax*. In years past, they set steel leg traps around Marmota holes, and they caught a bunch of 'em. It is a very exciting thing to catch a furry mammal with big teeth when you're a little boy. And when you get that first one, you're all fired up to get more. There is, of course, an adventure story to go with every critter that gets bagged.

Robert has, in days gone by, hunted woodchucks with a long, sharpened pole. He would stand back from the burrow entrance, waiting for the animal to emerge. Then, when it did, he jabbed at it with his spear. He got tufts of fur a few times but no complete woodchuck. A steel fence post and a forked stick (to pin the animal down) were also used without success. Imagine how thrilling it must be for a boy to wait, spear poised, in anticipation of the plump, brown and black creature showing itself, and then . . . *There it is!*

This summer the hunting is different. Robert and James, have moved beyond leg traps and spears. They use a Ruger .22 rifle, equipped with a scope and some "stinger" hollow point bullets. They hunt in the recently mowed hay field behind the wooded gully in back of our house.

So far this summer, the field has yielded 28 woodchucks to the older neighbor boy who uses a .270 rifle with a deluxe scope, a tripod, and bullets that cost almost a buck apiece. "The bullets are this long," Robert says, spreading his thumb and forefinger at least three inches apart.

Our rule is that the boys must ask permission to shoot the gun: "Dad, can I go hunting?" It is a request that delights me because I believe it is so good for a boy in the country to hunt woodchucks on a summer afternoon. But it is also a request that brings a pang of fear, and it moves me to whisper a prayer for a safe outing. I always tell them, "You be careful!" They have taken a good hunter safety course. They are very careful. But still, I tell them that every time, and I say the prayer.

The two brothers usually hunt together. I do not let James hunt alone unless I can see him from our property. They want to take two rifles but I only let them take the one. They also take the folding X-shaped bipod that Robert fashioned using 3/4-inch pine scraps from my shop. He cut sharp angles on the bottoms of the X so it won't move when it is set on the earth. He slings the bipod over his shoulder with a length of sisal twine. "It works good!" he proudly tells me.

Prior to this day, Robert and James have not been successful at gun hunting. They have been shooting at the animals and missing the mark. It is discouraging, and some boys would give up. But Robert has never been one to give up. He is persistent. He is determined. It is part of the way God made him.

Robert has worked over a period of many days to adjust the gun's optical sight. He does this by shooting from our backyard into a target on the other side of the gully. He clamps the gun into a makeshift rest he put together with yet more scrap wood. He also consulted with the neighbor boy about sighting in the gun and how to aim.

Today, the patience and persistence bore fruit. Robert and James were away in the hayfield hunting for well over an hour. It might have been two hours. It was long enough that I was beginning to wonder about them. Then I walked out onto the loading dock of my little workshop and there they were, my healthy, tanned blessings from the Lord, just coming to see me, gun in hand, sheathed knives on their hips, and big smiles on their faces.

"How was the hunting, guys?" I asked.

Robert replied first: "We shot four woodchucks, Dad."

I was taken aback . . . "Really?!"

"Yeah, and I can prove it," James said as he reached down to undo the cargo pocket flap on the side of his camouflage pants. He pulled out a handful of black woodchuck tails and laid them on the dock. One tail was noticeably bigger than the others. "I shot that big one, and Robert shot the other three."

They were proud hunters and I was duly impressed. Then came the stories of the hunt.

My suburbanized upbringing was much, much different than that of my sons. Once, when I was probably 12 years old, I discovered a woodchuck between the galvanized garbage cans in back of our little ranch house in the big housing development. I was moving the cans and there it was. It looked at me and it really shook me up. I did not know what it was. I had never seen a woodchuck before. I backed off slowly and ran like crazy to tell my mother about the beast.

My father was at work. My mother called a neighbor man who came over with a pistol. He walked up close and shot it twice. I watched as best as I could through a screened window from the safety of my home.

My sons are not helpless, sissified, geeky suburban Moderns, like I was. They would never run from a wood-chuck. They would capture it or club it, spear it or shoot it. At the very least they would sic the dog on it. And if the dog treed it (which she has done on a few occasions), they would work together to knock it from its perch.

They are not brutish agrarian boys. They do not torture or play with their prey; they kill it as quickly and humanely as they can, and they do not take delight in the killing. But they love the hunt.

Sometimes I wonder if maybe God created woodchucks for no other reason than to give boys experience at hunting. My sons are making glorious childhood memories while learning about woodchucks and guns and patience and persistence, and a whole lot more.

One day my sons will be men who, if necessary, will be capable of protecting their families. They will be able to put wild meat on the table. And they will be able to teach their sons, my grandchildren, these things. The way I see it, this is all very good.

19

The Theology of Food Independence

I'D LIKE TO BEGIN THIS ESSAY BY ASKING A personal question: If, tomorrow morning, you were no longer able to buy food from a grocery store, how long would you be able to feed your family?

That is the exact question I posed to Marlene recently, and it is, my dear reader, something I hope you will seriously consider for yourself.

You should ask yourself this question because the industrial food oligopoly is powerful and capable, but it is not sovereign. The probability of peak oil* and the assurance of higher energy costs means that food from corporations *will* be more expensive. Beyond that, natural disasters and geo-political happenings will make some or all corporate foods unavailable at times and in places. Disruptions in the food supply could be minor, short-lived, and localized, or they could be major, long-lasting (even permanent), and wide-spread. To depend on the industrial providers in the face of this reality is foolishness.

---

* The term "peak oil" refers to the Hubert Peak Theory, which was proposed by geophysicist M. King Hubert in 1956. Hubert postulated that every oil field has a functional lifespan and a maximum output point, which is the peak. Once the peak output is reached, production gradually tapers off. The remaining oil reserve also becomes progressively more difficult and more expensive to extract.

United States oil production peaked in 1971. Some analysts believe global oil production peaked in the spring of 2004. Other analysts dispute the 2004 date. But nobody disputes the fact that oil is a finite resource and peak will occur sometime in the 21st century, probably sooner than later.

It is an especially foolish thing for people who believe that the God of creation is sovereign Lord over all, for people who have a realistic understanding of the nature of God. So many Christians today look at Him and His Word like a can of mixed nuts: they pick out the pieces they like best and leave the rest.

For example, people like to say that God is love. Well, He surely is and the cross of Christ is more than sufficient proof of that. And God is certainly patient. But there is another side to His nature. God is also holy and righteous, and His patience has its limits. His Word says that God *hates* pride and arrogance. It says He executes His judgment on the nations—on those who turn their back on Him and His law and, worse yet, exalt themselves above Him.

That description sounds a lot like America in the beginning of the 21st century. And it describes very well the corporate-industrial system that now dominates the world today. Like Nimrod's Babylon, the powerful, centralized, corporate food system pridefully recognizes no sovereign God above itself.

The food oligarchy is now genetically manipulating and creating new plant seeds that are "better" than the ones God created—seeds that can be protected by patent and sold for great profit. The same is being done with animals.

God created and gave freely for His glory and the good of mankind. The industrial providers take God's creation unto themselves, recreate it for their own glory, and charge money for the good of their bottom line.

It is a brave new world that these pioneering sovereigns are creating to serve their own greedy purposes. And it is doomed. The great ziggurat of pride and profit that the industrial providers are building will crumble into ruins because God is God and they are not. He will allow the foolishness of men for a season. Then He will destroy their little kingdoms. You can count on it.

For Christians to put their full faith and hope in the provision of this industrial system that is in total rebellion against God is akin to participating in the rebellion.

Obedience to God calls for breaking the ties that bind us to ungodly industrialism. Obedience calls for us to grow our own food. This is why God Himself showed Adam how to plant the garden. And God says that if a man does not work, he should not eat. Do you see the connection?

Sure, it's hard to grow your own food. And it's harder yet to harvest and preserve it. And there are no guarantees that any crop will do well, that it will bear good fruit. This is the way God designed it and the reason why is pretty clear. The Homegrown Food System keeps us, as God's people, humble and dependent on Him, looking to Him for His blessings of provision.

What I am talking about here is fundamental, down-to-earth, biblical theology. I do not think God's word could be clearer on this matter. But you're not likely to hear it preached in your church.

So, back to the question of how long will your current food supply last . . . .

Am I suggesting, as some do, that Christians should stockpile industrial food (store-bought canned goods and military-style MREs maybe) to be ready for disaster and shortages? No, I am not.

Though I see nothing particularly wrong with that, what I am saying is something much more important, something much more life-changing, exciting, challenging, and reward-ing. I am saying that I believe Christians must understand how completely dependent they are on the ungodly culture around them for their daily sustenance. And, knowing this, they should begin to work harder towards providing for themselves, as much as possible, apart from industrialism.

It is through our own labors and harvests, in humble re-liance on God's blessings, that we should provide food for our families. We must do this because it is what He requires of us.

Because I am persuaded of the truth of what I've told you here, I am also personally convicted. I already grow some of my own food, but next spring, I will be growing more, and we will be preserving more. We will also continue to raise our own poultry.

We're even giving serious consideration to getting a couple of pigs this next spring. That will be a new adventure for us. We don't really eat much pork, but we'll eat a bit more and have a homegrown commodity that we can sell or trade with others in our community. I hope to expand my food growing efforts even more in the future when I am able to purchase more than the 1.5 acres of land I now have.

Food independence under God is not a destination. It is a journey. And like any journey, it requires a first step. Then it requires continued advancement. If you are also convicted of your need to break away from dependence on the ungodly providers, I wish you well on your journey.

⚜

Dr. Erwin Chargoff, eminent biochemist, often referred to as the father of molecular biology, warned that all innovation does not result in "progress." He once referred to genetic engineering as "a molecular Auschwitz" and warned that the technology of genetic engineering poses a greater threat to the world than the advent of nuclear technology. "I have the feeling that science has transgressed a barrier that should have remained inviolate," he wrote in his autobiography, Heraclitean Fire.
—Ignacio Chapela

⚜

Monsanto should not have to vouchsafe the safety of biotech food. Our interest is in selling as much of it as possible. Assuring its safety is the FDA's job.
—Phil Angell
Monsanto's Director of Corporate Communications

20

"Wanna Do the Farmer's Handshake?"

I HAVE TAUGHT MY SONS, AND I OFTEN REMIND them, about the importance of shaking hands like a man, even if they are only boys.

First, don't shake fingertips. Look at the other person's hand and sock yours deep into his, palm to palm. The grip should be firm. Not tight, but firm. And if you are shaking hands with a man who has a firm shake, meet it with at least equal "firmity." In other words, don't shake hands like a wimp.

Also, I have explained that it is vitally important to make a conscious effort to look the person whose hand you are shaking directly in the eyes. You can look into one eye, then the next, back and forth. Or, it is acceptable to focus your attention directly between the eyes. Of course, a friendly smile on the face is a necessary ingredient, too. This is one of those things that a father must teach his sons.

My boys have shaken a lot of hands. It is something we do in church. After the announcements and before the service begins, the congregation takes a few moments to get out of their seats and greet one another. A whole lot of handshaking ensues.

After church, on the ride home, my boys sometimes comment on the handshaking experiences of the morning. We've had many conversations about handshakes.

When one of my sons has done some small but significant thing, I extend my hand and we will shake. It is my way of acknowledging their initiative or accomplishment. On some occasions, once I have their hand and we've shaken, I'll pull them towards me and give a hug, too. This happened the other day.

Robert has been working quite a lot of afternoons on a neighboring farm, helping to load hay in the barn. He loves the hard work, and that pleases me.

So, when Robert came home, dirty from the chaff, and told me the farmer wants him to work three more afternoons later this week, I couldn't help but smile and put my hand out. "Good going, Robert!"

We shook and I held on tight. I said, "Wow, you're getting some big, hardworking man's hands there!" He was grinning. I gave him a hug. It was a nice moment.

Then, my youngest son, James, came up to me and asked, "Hey Dad, wanna do the farmer's handshake?"

I said, "What do you mean?"

He said, "Put your hands like this . . ." and he interlaced the fingers of both hands in front of him, with his palms facing him and his two thumbs straight up. I did the same.

"Now do this . . ." he said as he turned his hands so the palms were facing away, towards me. His arms were extended and his two thumbs were pointing down. I did the same.

As soon as my hands were in position, he unlocked his fingers, grabbed my thumbs and started giving them a milking. It was really cute and I got a big laugh out of it.

It turns out that an older man at church taught James this special farmer's handshake. I think every kid should know it. Pass it on.

A hug is a handshake from the heart.
—Unknown

21

Christian-Agrarian Revival

I N THE EARLY TO MID 1800s, THE INDUSTRIAL Revolution started to elbow itself onto the world stage. It became a steam roller that eventually crushed every vital vestige of agrarian culture. Prior to that time, the majority of people on this earth had lived within the agrarian paradigm.

All things were remade in the industrial image. It started, innocently enough, with manufacturing. Then followed the inexorable industrialization of government, the military, education, science, medicine, economics, agriculture, and even the church.

As a result of industrialism, the ancient and accepted structure of the family was slowly ripped from its traditional foundations. First, the family was emasculated when industrial factories lured fathers from their fields and home-centered cottage industries. Soon, children were attending government schools to be educated, then mothers entered the workplace. With the homes thus emptied, no one was around to tend to the sick and elderly, so they were shuttled into industrial institutions of care.

A plethora of social ills followed this fracturing of the family. And a plethora of industrial solutions arose to address the ills. Each solution created more problems, thus demanding more solutions.

Another result of industrialism's relentless march toward more control and even greater industrialism, was the destruction of close-knit local communities and the localized economy of those communities. The environment was a casualty, too. With government blessing, corporate entities showed their contempt for creation by ravaging the land and waters, like no one before could have ever imagined.

The Moderns will argue that industrialism has been good, or, at least, much more good than bad. They believe the industrial lie: that men and the political, scientific, social, military, and medical inventions of men will eventually solve all problems. In other words, that greater industrialism is the cure for lesser industrialism. The Moderns know nothing better.

What these Moderns fail to see is that, in exchange for temporary comfort and cheap, plentiful stuff, they become wards of the industrial providers. Furthermore, they do not see industrialism poisoning their minds and bodies. They eagerly accept the false promises of the providers. As a result, they never realize the fullness of life lived as God intended it to be lived.

However, more and more, the Moderns are being filled with a sense of dread as the industrial era approaches its apogee. An era of reckoning will follow. It must happen. Prideful industrialism has sown the seeds of its own destruction. The Moderns will face this eventuality with the grace of a deer standing in the middle of the highway at night, transfixed by the headlights of an onrushing tractor trailer.

I don't know how the industrial era will collapse, only that it will. My guess is that a worldwide economic crisis will be a major part of the story. It is only fitting since industrialism in all its many forms is rooted in greed and the love of money.

I don't know if the industrial era will end with a bang, similar to the Twin Towers of the World Trade Center, crashing to rubble under their own weight. Perhaps it will end in a slow, almost imperceptible, then gasping, then whimpering, decline.

Neither do I know when the industrial era will end. The beginning of the end may be in my lifetime. Maybe we are already in the beginning of the end. Or it could be something my descendants will have to deal with.

Only God knows how the demise of the industrial era will be played out. That's because He is sovereign. He knows the beginning from the end. He directs the events of history for His own purposes, primary of which is to bring glory to Himself.

I have said all this to set the stage for discussing something far more important than the imminent death of industrialism. Throughout the trials and tribulations of history, God has always been faithful to preserve a remnant of His people. I believe He is doing this even now. His spirit is moving, calling His flock to live very differently from the modern world *and* the modern church. He is calling a people to live, in the words of R.C. Sproul, Jr., "simple, separate, and deliberate lives to the glory of God and for the building of His kingdom."

A portion of His flock has been and continues to be called to a movement that I believe is best described as Christian agrarian revival. It is not an organized movement in the industrial sense. There is no carefully planned, well-funded, centralized campaign. There is no denominational backing. There is no National Association of Christian Agrarian Revival.

Major news media are not making a sensation of this movement. They do not even see it. But it is happening. It has been happening. God is setting the stage, moving His people into position now for His future purposes. This is a heaven-directed, from-the-bottom-up movement.

The rise of Christian homeschooling had a lot to do with all of this. Then God started turning the hearts of fathers back to their children, back to biblical fatherhood. Now He is leading families back to the land, back to home and home-centered enterprises that keep the family together, back to an agrarian way of life that is more dependent on Him and less dependent on the industrial providers.

Those of God's people who are doing these things are doing them with an eye to the future, with an eye towards establishing strong, thriving, interdependent families and local communities. These people will stand in the days of adversity. What they have done (indeed, what they are doing even now) will shine like a beacon, showing the dying culture around them that there is hope in the midst of the chaos. Do you see it?

*There seem to be but three ways for a nation
to acquire wealth. The first is by war, as the
Romans did, in plundering their neighbors. This
is robbery. The second by commerce, which is generally
cheating. The third is by agriculture,
the only honest way, wherein man receives a
real increase of the seed thrown into the ground,
in a kind of continual miracle, wrought by the
hand of God in his favor, as a reward for his
innocent life and his virtuous industry.*
—Benjamin Franklin

*"Some day," old Jamie had said,
"there will come a reckoning and the country
will discover that farmers are more necessary than
traveling salesmen, that no nation can exist or
have any solidity which ignores the land.
But it will cost the country dear."*
—Louis Bromfield
The Farm

22

"Annie's Got a Raccoon!"

L AST CHRISTMAS I BOUGHT MY TWO OLDEST sons, Chaz and Robert, a New England Firearms, 20-gauge, break-action, single-shot shotgun. They are well-made guns and a good value for around $100 each. If properly cared for, they should last at least one lifetime. Guns are a perfect gift for a dad to give his sons.

I intended to buy James, my youngest, the same gun. In fact, I ordered three guns at the same time. But when I went to pick them up, the store had sold one. So I missed out on giving each of my boys the same model of gun with three consecutive serial numbers. As a result, James did not get his first gun last Christmas. He will get it this Christmas.

I chose the NEF 20-gauge because our whole family took a hunter safety class last fall, and the instructor recommended that particular gun as ideal for a boy's first firearm. A boy can use a 20-gauge to shoot birds, squirrels, and even big game like deer. He can also shoot a raccoon, which leads me to the case in point.

Robert and James roam the woods and fields and streams around our house almost every day when the weather is good, and many days when it isn't. Often they have a gun with them. Such was the case yesterday with James, who turned 11 last month.

James was out with his brother's 20-gauge in the woods just behind our house. He was watching and waiting for a squirrel to show itself. I was home from work for the day doing some remodeling inside the house. Marlene was in the kitchen. Robert was busy upstairs.

All of a sudden, Robert came running down the stairs. He loudly exclaimed, "Annie's got a raccoon in the woods!" and breezed out the door. Annie, I should explain, is our faithful mixed-breed dog that we got from the pound a few years ago.

Marlene and I ran out behind Robert. As we neared the edge of the woods, a shotgun blast echoed out of the gully. At the sound, I ran faster.

Seconds later I found James standing at the bottom of the steep embankment that leads down to the creek. About five feet away, in the water, was the bloody carcass of a good-sized raccoon. It was laying on its back, slowly, reflexively writhing as the last bit of life ebbed from its body. The dog was standing over the coon. The boy seemed calm and collected. The father and mother were much relieved.

What had happened? Well, evidently James saw the dog take off down over the bank and heard the ensuing fight. Annie makes a distinctive moaning-yelp of a sound when she is engaged in mortal combat. I have only heard the haunting cry once before when she attacked and, after a savage battle, eventually managed to kill a feral cat in a hedgerow across from our house. But the kids have heard the sound on numerous other occasions. Robert heard it from upstairs in our house and assumed the dog had a coon.

Naturally, James ran down to the fight. Annie had the critter by the head in a pool of water. James closed the hinge-action on the gun, aimed it, and yelled for Annie to "*Git!*" The dog backed off and James fired.

One shot, square into the neck and chest at close range with a load of #6, and that coon was done for.

Annie's head was bloodied. She had cuts around her nose and mouth. I put some rubber gloves on. I stroked her and praised her.

Episodes like that make a mongrel country dog's life worth living. Annie was battle-scarred but more alive than any coddled city mutt could dream of being, and she would live to fight another day.

This daylight coon James and Annie bagged yesterday was probably sick. I'd guess it had rabies. That's why I wore gloves. Tonight Marlene took Annie for a ride to Doc Mackey for a rabies booster shot.

Doc Mackey has been a vet in these parts pretty much forever. He is man of few words and most folks around here have a Doc Mackey story. A fellow who used to work for me told me about the time he took his coon dog to Doc. The dog's breath smelled absolutely horrible, and the guy was afraid something was seriously wrong with the animal. Doc Mackey put his nose down by the dog's mouth and took a sniff. Then he muttered his prognosis: "Been eatin' dead."

As for the raccoon, we went back to the scene of the fracas awhile later and it was gone. I suspect Annie hauled it off somewhere and half-buried it. I suppose, in the mind of the dog, the job isn't done until the animal is buried. It's probably in my garden. It wouldn't be the first time I forked up one of her conquests.

❧

How many parents have tried in vain to prevent little Timmy from playing with guns? Give it up. If you do not supply a boy with weapons, he will make them from whatever materials are at hand. My boys chew their graham crackers into the shape of hand guns at the breakfast table. Every stick or fallen branch is a spear, or better, a bazooka. Despite what many modern educators would say, this is not a psychological disturbance brought on by violent television or chemical imbalance. Aggression is part of the masculine design; [men] are hardwired for it. If we believe that man is made in the image of God, then we would do well to remember that "The LORD is a warrior; the LORD is his name" (Exodus 15:3).
—John Eldredge
Wild at Heart

Thorns may hurt you, men may desert you,
sunlight turn to fog; but you're
never friendless ever, if you have a dog.
—Douglas Mallock

❦

He is your friend, your partner, your defender,
your dog. You are his life, his love, his leader.
He will be yours, faithful and true,
to the last beat of his heart.
You owe it to him to be worthy of such devotion.
—Unknown

❦

Recollect that the Almighty, who gave
the dog to be companion of our pleasures
and our toils, hath invested him with
a nature noble and incapable of deceit.
—Sir Walter Scott

❦

Dogs' lives are too short.
It is their only fault, really.
—Agnes Sligh Turnbull

❦

Personally, I would not give a fig for
any man's religion whose horse, cat and dog
do not feel its benefits.
—S. Parkes Cadman

23

The Life and Death of a Good Dog

YEARS AGO, AFTER MARLENE AND I MOVED into our humble, homemade, and only partially completed house in the countryside, we awoke one day to find a puppy outside our door. It was brown and black, furry and cute. The morning was autumn frosty and the poor little creature was whimpering. We figured it had been dropped off in the night by someone with more puppies than they knew what to do with.

So we brought the tiny wayfarer into our home. We found that it was a she. We fed her and loved her and we gave her the proper name of "Pilgrim." For short, we just called her "Pilly."

She was a "Heinz 57." That's what a friend of mine calls mixed breed dogs. They are, to my way of thinking, the hardiest and best kind of dogs. Judging from her eventual size and shape, she looked to have a good measure of German Shepherd in her.

When spring rolled around, my neighbor up the road stopped by one day and, noticing Pilgrim, commented that she looked a lot like his dog. I told him about how she showed up one morning back in the fall and we took her in. He said his dog had a litter of puppies back in the fall and the runt had come up missing. So that's where our Pilgrim came from. She was the runt of the litter. How she found her way down the hill to our door remains a mystery.

Pilgrim grew up to be a wonderful pet. Like all good country dogs, she dutifully and properly announced visitors and intruders by barking. But she did not bark excessively at all hours, or yap hysterically as some canines are wont to do.

She was neither a hunter nor scrapper, but she didn't hesitate to do battle with woodchucks that dared to enter our yard and my garden. She did not chase cars and she did not jump up on people. But the dog was not perfect; she had one particularly annoying habit.

Sometimes, early in the morning, from her bed in the kitchen, Pilgrim would howl. When it first happened, and we were startled from our peaceful slumber, we responded by running downstairs, scolding her and whacking her with a newspaper.

She got the idea pretty quick that we did not like howling in the wee hours of the morning. But still, when the urge came upon her, she howled. It was something that she could not contain. She would try her best to hold it back because she did not want to be scolded and paper-whacked. But eventually her suppressed little moans would erupt into full-fledged howls. What brought it on was never clear.

Fortunately, it was not an every morning occurrence, and in time, we simply tolerated it. The fault could be overlooked because Pilgrim was an otherwise fine dog with a gentle disposition, and as is the case with such dogs, she loved us unconditionally. She also liked to take rides.

On one memorable occasion, I was cruising down the state highway into town with Pilgrim in the back of my pickup truck. As I rounded a bend in the road I heard a sound from behind that caused me to look in the rear-view mirror. I was horrified to see ol' Pilly hurtling headlong through the air. She landed on her side, hard against the gravelly shoulder of the road. With a cloud of stone dust trailing behind, she violently barrel-rolled into the front lawn of a farm house.

I slammed on the brakes, threw the truck into reverse, and figured that if my dog wasn't dead, she was surely going to be badly broken. I got out of the truck dreading what I was going to have to deal with, but to my utter amazement, Pilgrim came trotting around the back bumper towards me.

I couldn't believe my eyes. She was a little excited, maybe confused, but seemingly okay. I think I was more upset about the whole thing than she. When I opened the front passenger door, she hopped right up into the seat and gave me one of those big, openmouthed, tongue-hanging dog smiles.

After a few years, Marlene started having babies and Pilgrim did not get as much of our attention as before. But she was okay with that. She tolerated the curious children that grew up around her, and she was their ever-vigilant protector. She really was a special dog to us.

The years passed all too quickly and Pilgrim became old and feeble. Hip dysplasia set in. The disease worsened to the point that she could no longer walk. We could not care for her in that condition and we were faced with the sad reality that it was time to end her life.

Doc Mackey, the old country vet who had always taken care of Pilgrim when the need arose, was on vacation. A sign outside his office read, "Gone Fishin'" That meant he was probably visiting his son in Alaska. So Marlene called another veterinarian. She found out it would cost $65 to euthanize a dog. Disposal of the body would cost more.

I had a shovel, a strong back, and the land to give my dog a proper burial. But, sadly, I did not have $65 to spare. We were making due with my one income from carpentry work and money was real tight. That's when it entered my mind that I would do the unthinkable. I would shoot my own dog.

The killing of animals is a regular part of life on a homestead. Some animals are killed for their meat, some are killed for their furs, some are killed because they are a nuisance or a threat. In all of these cases, the killing is relatively easy once you've done it a few times. That is, however, not the case when it comes to ending the life of your own beloved dog.

My friend, Steve, offered to take Pilgrim away and do the dirty deed for me. I imagine it is much easier to kill someone else's dog. I thanked him, but as a man, I felt I needed to do it myself.

What did farmers and woodsmen of old do when it was time to end their dog's life and there was no veterinarian with a needle? They did it themselves, with a gun. Properly done, it is quick and painless. At least, for the dog it is painless. No man is comfortable with the thought of killing his dog.

We told our children that Pilgrim was old and suffering and she needed to be "put to sleep." They took it well. Robert was nine years old at the time, and he helped me dig a grave in the woods behind our house. Then Marlene went with the kids to her mother's place for a few hours. She knew what I planned to do but the boys thought I would be taking Pilgrim to the veterinarian while they were gone.

I took my .22 rifle to the grave, chambered a round, and set it on the ground. Then I went back to the house for Pilgrim. I spent some time with her. I stroked her head and neck and scratched behind her ears and told her what a good dog she had been. The sun was setting lower in the sky, and I needed to be doing what I had set my mind to do.

With one arm around her chest and the other around her back end, I lifted Pilgrim up like a farmer lifts a newborn calf. I hugged her body tight to my chest and carried her into the woods, all the while assuring her that she was a good dog and everything was okay. I set her down next to the hole in the ground.

On my knees in front of her, the gun on the ground behind me, I gave her more praise and attention, and I prayed that the Lord would help me, that Pilgrim would not suffer. Her back end was limp on the ground, her front legs held her torso up; she was looking intently at me. I reached for the rifle and clicked the safety off.

With my heart pounding hard in my chest, I stood, trembling. I positioned the end of the barrel a couple inches away from the shallow indent in the center of her skull, just above her eyes. I did not hold it there long. She did not know what was about to happen. Her eyes, fixed on mine, showed nothing but love and trust.

It was over and done in an instant. God was merciful to us both.

Everything in the woods was, by then, a shadow in the gray twilight. All the gut-wrenching emotions I had been suppressing came to the surface. Anguish. Fear. Sorrow. Relief. Regret. I grabbed my shovel, flipped the lifeless body into the hole, and furiously filled it in. I topped the mound with a few big rocks I had gathered for that purpose. Then, out of breath and exhausted, I walked back to the house. It was finished.

Awhile later Marlene returned with the children. She came in the door and gave me that "did-you-do-it" look. I nodded my head slowly. She said, "I don't want to know anything about it." My boys asked if I had taken Pilgrim to the vet. I responded that she had been "put to sleep" and that she did not suffer and that I had buried her in the woods. That was good enough for them, and as I write this, they have never known otherwise.

Many people in our modern culture believe that animals are people and people are animals. Such folks fail to see any difference because they refuse to believe in the God of Genesis, the One who created people and animals and everything else.

Scripture says that man was created in God's image and that we were created to have a relationship with Him. Animals were not created in God's image and they do not have the desire or ability to know God. That is the difference and it is a significant one. It is something I have explained to my children many times.

God has given mankind dominion over the animals. This does not mean that we are to treat them poorly. On the contrary, the dominion mandate brings responsibility. We are called to use animals responsibly and to treat them humanely, which means with compassion and sympathy. But it does not mean to treat them like humans.

And the Lord God
planted a garden eastward in Eden.
—Genesis 2:8

※

And the Lord God took the
man and put him into the
garden of Eden
to dress it and to keep it
—Genesis 2:15

※

For thou shalt eat the labour of
thine hands: happy shalt thou be,
and it shall be well with thee
—Psalm 128:2

※

If ye walk in my statutes, and
keep my commandments, and do them;
Then will I give you rain in due season,
and the land shall yield her increase,
and the trees of the field shall yield their fruit.
And your threshing shall reach unto
the vintage, and the vintage shall reach unto
the sowing time; and ye shall eat your bread
to the full, and dwell in your land safely.
—Leviticus 26:3-5

24

I'm a Backslidden and Repentant Gardener

(Part One of The Autumn Trilogy)

THERE IS A TIME AND A SEASON FOR EVERY-
thing, and yesterday it was time for me to return to
my garden. I had been away far too long—the whole
summer, in fact. Neglected as it was, the land that con-
stitutes my garden had become a dense jungle of weeds.

That is what happens when you don't tend your garden,
when you fail to exercise dominion as you should. The
weeds take root and grow huge. They rob sunlight and
nutrients and the good seed is unable to grow to its full potential. It is a sad thing to see this happen and to know that
it has happened because you have been an unfaithful
steward.

But God is merciful to backslidden and repentant gar-
deners like me. He gives us another chance—next year. I
have that hope and the fresh enthusiasm that comes with
the thought of springtime and another growing season.

My absence from the garden was not due to sloth. It was
a result of a competing interest and my lack of time. I
needed to work on my house.

There were new windows and a door to put in. Siding to
put on. Painting to be done. A small addition had to be
built to provide more much-needed, room for my family. I
framed, roofed, insulated, wired, sheetrocked, wallpapered,
and made tremendous progress.

I know how to do that kind of work. I made my living
doing it for more than 20 years. I am comfortable with the
tools and processes of building and remodeling. I have
taught others these things. I have even written magazine

articles and three how-to books. But I do not enjoy it anymore. I would rather toil in my garden. I would rather plant and tend a vineyard, raise Dexter cattle, grow blueberries, manage a wood lot, and so much else!

My great agrarian vision is to have more land—land where my children can work with me and develop their own agrarian interests; land where my grandchildren can play and explore, learn and grow; land where I can live a full life closer to creation and the Sovereign Creator I serve; land where I can die knowing that the Christian agrarian values and beliefs I hold dear have been passed on and embraced by my children, and that they will, in turn, be passed on to the children that follow.

The thought of grandchildren—many of them—delights me. God willing, I will live to see them, to know them, to love them, to give them my time, to make a difference in their lives, to be an old and wise and beloved grandfather, an agrarian patriarch. I think about these things. These are some of the most important things in life.

Yes, I made tremendous progress on the house. Last week I installed green shutters by the windows. It was the crowning touch. Marlene stood beside me looking at the shutters, and she remarked with obvious pleasure that, after 20 years of plywood, tar paper, and partial siding, it finally looked like a "real house."

And so it does. At least, it does on the one side that is completely done. There still remains much to do. I will make more progress next year but the hardest work is over. It is downhill from here. Next year the house will look even better. It will be even more marketable. That is the objective. And next year I will be able to do better with my garden.

Marlene says that next year she and I should get up early every morning and spend a half hour working in the garden together before I have to leave for my non-agrarian regular job. I do not know if this will actually happen, but I am so blessed to have a wife who is thinking this way. It is a biblical concept—the man and his helpmeet, the woman God has given him, working together to tend the garden. We should do that. Yes, we really should!

And, knowing how I feel, she consoles me about the jungle that was once my well-kempt Eden. I have not gone there but she has bushwacked her way into it all summer and come out with a steady supply of food. It was not the garden it should have been; there was not an abundant bounty—but it fed us remarkably well. Nevertheless, I will do better next year, and that is why I returned to my garden yesterday. Yesterday I did battle. . . .

⚘

If it's drama that you sigh for,
plant a garden and you'll get it.
You will know the thrill of battle
fighting foes that will beset it.
—Edward A. Guest
Plant a Garden

⚘

I sought a piece of land which I
could love passionately, which I could
spend the rest of my life
cultivating, cherishing, and improving,
which I might leave together, perhaps,
with my own feeling for it,
to my children who might in time
leave it to their children.
—Louis Bromfield
Pleasant Valley

There is more beauty in a single
flower than could adorn all the
greatest cathedrals in the world.
—John Ruskin

⚜

Until man duplicates a blade of grass,
nature can laugh at his so-called
scientific knowledge . . . It's
obvious that we don't know one
millionth of one percent about anything.
—Thomas Alva Edison

⚜

I love to think of nature as an
unlimited broadcasting station through
which God speaks to us every hour,
if we will only tune in.
—George Washington Carver

⚜

Every flower of the field, every
fiber of a plant, every particle
of an insect carries with it
the impress of its Maker and
can—if duly considered—read
us lectures of ethics or divinity.
—Sir Thomas Pope Blount

25

The Battle and the Victory

(Part Two of The Autumn Trilogy)

A
S I MENTIONED IN THE PREVIOUS STORY, I planted and cared for my garden only a short while earlier this year before abandoning it to focus on more pressing projects. Forsaken as it was, weeds overtook the garden. Amazingly, it still yielded a decent harvest, but it was not as good as it could have been and I felt justly shamed, as would any sincere agrarian.

Shame comes from conviction that works in the heart of a man who has the conscience to be convicted. And, if it is true, such conviction should naturally translate into some form of repentant action. That is why the day before yesterday, I awoke with resolute determination: before the sun set that day, I would retake the land I had lost to the invading vegetation.

Though it was a formidable quest, I was undaunted by the tall, dense fortress of foliage. I'm certain that some men would have been intimidated. Such a task could well lead to second thoughts. I can imagine their thinking: "Perhaps it might be better for me to wait for another day, and instead, spend this day entertaining myself with some vacuous modern amusement."

Ha! Such cowardly thoughts!

There is no way I will shrink from this task. I see not the weeds standing tall and strong. I see glorious victory. I see the enemy plucked from his stronghold with brute strength and violence. I see the dying carcasses heaped tall and rotting into compost. This day *shall not* pass without me reestablishing dominion over this land.

I am certain of my victory because I have battled this vegetative foe before. I know his weakness, and I have waited for just the right time to launch my redemptive attack.

The past summer was long and dry, and the soil became very hard. Roots are firmly anchored in such land. But the rain has come. Two days of it. My rain gauge tells me 2-1/2 inches has fallen. The sandy loam is soaked through. The ground is now soft. The enemy is vulnerable. This enemy shall be delivered into my hand on this day. Of this, there is no doubt.

And the weather on this day of conquest suits me. There is a low, dense cover of gray clouds. Fog is slowly moving. Its mist is cool and palpable. The foliage is dripping wet. It is a primordial-like atmosphere.

My feet, shod with tall, slip-on rubber boots, will stay warm and dry. Old jeans, a hooded sweatshirt, and a baseball cap complete my battle dress. I have gloves. A utility knife is in my back pocket. A garden cart is by my side. It is all I will need.

There are 24 precisely arranged beds in my garden. A walkway, two-feet wide, separates them. Each bed will be an arena of battle.

With my cart beside me, I begin to lay siege. I bend at the waist, reach down under the wet canopy of a giant green and red pigweed. I am looking for the the base, the primary artery that feeds this monster. When I find it, I grasp the stiff stalk firmly and give a sure, steady pull. Behemoth resists momentarily, but to no avail. The soft soil releases its grip. This beast has met its match. There is something incredibly satisfying about pulling on a large weed, and having it, roots and all, come free of the earth. I pull another and another. Even the dandelions with their long taproots pull completely free.

My garden cart fills to overflowing quickly.

It occurs to me that pulling weeds from the soil of my garden on a damp, misty day in October is not a chore. It is not drudgery. I am where I should be, doing that which I should be doing. I am once again tending the garden. I have returned to the work that I was designed to do. It is a good feeling. A very good feeling.

26

Rediscovery
and Remembrance

(Part Three of The Autumn Trilogy)

I T IS AN OCTOBER DAY WITH FOG, MIST, AND NO
sunshine. I am pulling the weeds from my garden beds.
The soil is wet from heavy rains that have come and
gone. Every weed, roots and all, is mine for the pulling.

The work is not hard but there are *many* carts full of
weeds to remove, and I am bent over much of the time. I will
finish the job I have set before myself but it is tiring. At 47
years of age, I'm sorry to say that I'm not the physical spec-
imen I once was. I'm not as limber. Not as toned. Not as
strong. That bothers me.

I think to myself how strong I was as a younger man. I
think to myself how young men delight in the strength of
their youth. I think to myself that old men delight in the
memory of how strong they once were. And what of middle-
aged men like me? We're looking back and looking forward
and just trying to hold on to what we have, to not let it slip
away. I would be so much stronger and healthier if I
worked in the garden like this every day. If it didn't kill me,
it would make me stronger.

I am clearing out a bed that was planted to green beans. I
remember how, back in the spring, Marlene told me to be
sure to plant lots of beans this year, and I did. She steamed
them whole and put butter on them. I like to pick buttered
green beans up with my fingers, one at a time then, head
tipped up and chin jutted out, feed them down into my
mouth. I realize it's not considered good manners to do this.
But it seems only right and proper with fresh-from-the-
garden, steamed green beans.

There, under the weeds, I find over-mature, browned
pods. Some have split open and spilled reddish beans on
the ground. They are swollen from the rain and have developed a small, white, tail-like sprout.

My mind drifts back to elementary school where we soaked bean seeds and watched them grow. I think of a girl I knew named Margaret Keegan who, on the first day of second grade, while standing in the lunch line, told the teacher that she wanted to be called Penny. She said this at the exact same time I happened to be looking down at the shiny pennies I had slipped into the leather of my new loafers.

I have not thought of that girl or that moment in years. I've made my way from green beans to Margaret Keegan in, probably, a matter of seconds. That's the way the mind works. It drifts erratically and unpredictably and very quickly from one thing to another. At least, that's the way mine works.

I'm at another weed-infested bed and I can't recall what I planted here. But I see a leathery-looking skin and it comes back to me. This was the cantaloupe bed. My son Robert wanted to grow cantaloupes. I explained to him that cantaloupes need nutrient-rich soil. So we put a shovel-full of compost under each seedling before planting it. Then we put wire hoops and plastic over the bed to make a little greenhouse. The plants grew lush and thick and sprawled into the walkways.

I think that the last thing I did in this garden before abandoning it was to remove the plastic so bees could pollinate the flowers. Robert harvested picture-perfect and legendary-sweet melons from this mini-patch.

This garden bed has given my son a life lesson. He learned that he can grow awesome-good melons himself—that, in fact, the only awesome-good melons are the ones you grow yourself. I predict that this boy will, as a result of this experience, be planting and harvesting his own melons for years to come. And all future melons will be judged against this year's crop. They really were that good.

All of a sudden (I'm not sure how or why), I remember the lavender. I'm looking over my garden, trying to remember where, in the jungle of weeds, it is. I must see how my lavender plants have fared after my neglect.

I come upon the bed with lavender and I can see the plants have struggled to survive. I clear away the weeds and discover one plant has died. Four live, but they are green only on the tops. Down where the weeds closed in and the sun could not penetrate, the foliage has browned. A single, slender, flower stem with lonely lavender blossoms rises above the besieged plants.

I cannot pass by lavender without picking a sprig of leaves, crushing it between my fingers, and holding it to my nose. Today the scent is different than I remember. It reminds me of something from my past. Long ago, even before Margaret Keegan.

I close my eyes and my mind takes me to another place. I remember the place, but it was not a place with lavender, and this confuses me. I take another sprig, crush the blue-green leaves and breathe in slower, deeper, more deliberately.

I drift back in time to when I was a little boy at my grandparents' camp on Cross Lake in Northern Maine. I was walking into the old, dark boat house. There was a varnished wooden boat, life preservers, an outboard motor, a workbench with some tools and paintbrushes, and the smell of turpentine. The lavender leaves smell like turpentine to me! How strange. Yet it is true. It is unmistakable.

A fragrance can trigger remembrances like nothing else, and so it is with this lavender-cum-turpentine. My mind skips to another old remembrance . . . .

I must have been four years old. I was, once again, at my grandparents' camp. I remember it as if in a dream. I think my father was painting. It was on the porch, by the kitchen door. He was telling me that my mother and I would be going away and I would not see him for awhile. I was just listening. I was not upset. I did not understand.

Shortly thereafter, my mother and I went to California to live with an uncle. Later we came back east, to Springfield, Massachusetts. We lived in a complex of brick apartment buildings, she and I, and she worked at a *Friendly's* restaurant as a waitress. It was there that she met another man and she married him. He became my new father.

The next time I saw my first father was years later at my grandmother's house. I was visiting for the summer. My father had another wife and two children. He was *their* father. We have met a few times in the decades since and we are friendly (why wouldn't we be?), but I don't really know him. How odd. I'm thankful that my sons have never experienced this kind of situation.

I open my eyes and reach for the lone flower stem. Does it too smell of turpentine? I crush it and hold it to my nose. Ahhhh . . . now *that's* lavender! This last flower of the season must be the sweetest of all. But the pleasure of its scent is so fleeting.

As I am pulling weeds from the bed where I planted peppers, I come across a small bumblebee. It is on a broad pepper leaf. The black and yellow hairs on its back arc wet and ruffled. They look as though they've been spiked with some sort of hair gel. Brylcreem comes to mind. "A Little Dab'll Do Ya!" This, like penny loafers, surely dates me.

The insect's wings are ragged on the edges. The pollen sacs on its hind legs are packed and polished smooth. The pollen is such a bright yellow that it almost appears to glow amidst the hues of earth and late-season greenery.

This poor bee is not going anywhere for now. It is waiting for sunshine to come out and dry it off. I reach my gloved hand down to pick it up. I place it in the palm of my other hand, intending to observe it better.

But the tired bug summons its reserves. It buzzes in frantic circles and falls over the edge of my hand. It can not fly up and away, but it manages a respectable drop, down and over, onto a bush of sage in the adjoining bed. I wish the bee well and return to my work.

The soil in my garden is teeming with life. The earthworms always get my attention. They are there in abundance because my soil is rich with organic matter. The worms feed on it and leave castings which are the best natural fertilizer in the world. The weeds I am picking, so many cart loads of them, will be composted and returned to these beds, where the earthworms will have their way with them.

Earthworms come up with the roots of the weeds I pull. They are wriggling in the soil of the craters that remain. They are even coming up out of holes in the undisturbed surface of the earth and stretching out, as if they want to escape from impending disaster.

I love to see earthworms in my garden. The sight of them makes me think of Aristotle who said that earthworms are the intestines of the earth. And that makes me think of the homeschool lesson where we learned the names of the three great Greek philosophers. Aristotle is one. Who are the other two? Ah yes, now I remember: Socrates and Plato. And Plato makes me think of playdough. And playdough makes me think of bread dough. And bread dough makes me think of Marlene's homemade oatmeal bread. And that makes me think that I have worked up quite an appetite pulling these weeds. . . .

And so it was that I took a break from my labors and headed to the house for a little something to eat.

This story has been but a small sampling of my garden thoughts from that day of pulling weeds. Isn't it amazing where your mind will take you when you are working in your garden?

Smells detonate softly in our memory
like poignant land mines hidden
under the weedy mass of years.
Hit a tripwire of smell and memories
explode all at once. A complex vision
leaps out of the undergrowth.
—Diane Ackerman,
A Natural History of the Senses

Reduce the complexity of life by
eliminating the needless wants of life,
and the labors of life reduce themselves.
—Edwin Teale

❦

The sculptor produces the beautiful
statue by chipping away such parts
of the marble block as are not
needed—it is a process of elimination.
—Elbert Hubbard

❦

It is the simple things of life that make
living worthwhile, the sweet fundamental
things such as love and duty, work and rest,
and living close to nature. There are not
hothouse blossoms that can compare in beauty
and fragrance with my bouquet of wildflowers.
—Laura Ingalls Wilder

❦

My riches consist not in
the extent of my possessions
but in the fewness of my wants.
—J. Botherton

❦

How many things are there
which I do not want?
—Socrates

27

Making
Peppermint Tea

SEVERAL YEARS AGO, ONE OF MY NEIGHBORS spaded up from her garden a single clump of soil studded with healthy peppermint plants and gave it to me. I took the clump home, put it into a spade-size hole in the earth, packed soil around it, and added water. A lush patch of peppermint grew up in what seemed like no time at all. As a matter of fact, it grew and spread like a proverbial weed. I decided I would pick some of it to dry, and make a supply of tea.

It was a sunny summer morning, after the dew was off the leaves, when I stood at the edge of my peppermint patch, inspecting and plucking the choicest of stems. You know the choicest of peppermint stems when you see them. They are the ones with clean, perfect foliage. If a stem of leaves is old and faded, badly bug-eaten, or splattered by a bird dropping, it will not be one of the chosen ones. And you want to make certain that tiny translucent garden spiders have not wrapped and sealed their hapless prey with silky white webbing on the underside of the leaves you select.

It will typically be the top six to ten inches of fresh, new growth that meets these high standards. I made sure that I chose only the best-leafed stems that day.

As I was working, and I might add, thoroughly enjoying myself, I thought about those colorful, cellophane-wrapped boxes of peppermint tea bags in the supermarket. I wondered if someone like me judiciously eyes every stem for perfection before plucking it from the plant and drying it for tea. What an absurd thought that was.

Supermarket tea is made by a big company that judiciously eyes its bottom line. Careful hand selection is not efficient, and therefore, not profitable. No food-producing corporation can possibly survive in our industrial economy by providing only the very best product to the masses. Peppermint tea is but one example of this.

I think it is safe to say that store-bought peppermint tea is harvested by some sort of mechanical mower that cuts the entire plant, a whole field of it. What about the bird poop and the little bugs? No problem. Salmonella and other avian-transmitted pathogens, which are sometimes present in the errant droppings of passing birds, can probably be killed by blasting the plants with irradiation. How perfectly industrial!

Never mind that, within the food being irradiated, gamma rays create free radicals and unique new chemical compounds that have never adequately been studied for safety. The most important thing is that everything gets thoroughly killed.

Post-harvest fumigating of herbs used for teas is also a common practice. One popular fumigant, Phostoxin, is a great insecticide. It's so good, in fact, that it's also used to kill groundhogs! Doesn't that make you feel better about drinking those store-bought herbal teas? But, wait . . . how do they remove all the little vermin after they've so effectively gassed them to death? Perhaps it's best that *everything* is cut fine and tucked into those little bags.

And where exactly does all that peppermint in all those tea bags in all those colorful boxes on all those shelves in all those supermarkets all over the world come from? Who grew it? Who handled it? Was it sprayed with herbicides, fungicides, or pesticides when it was in the field? Was the soil it was grown in truly fertile and healthy or was it artificially enhanced for one more season with applications of petrochemical fertilizers?

Was sewage sludge with its toxic heavy metal concentrations (or, perhaps, something even more sinister) ever dumped on and mixed into the soil that grew the peppermint that came from who-knows-where?

Was the harvested plant put in a dryer immediately after harvest, or did it sit in a big clump somewhere and start to develop mold before it finally got to the dryer? Do gamma rays and Phostoxin kill mold, too?

So many questions and so few answers. What do we really know about all that nicely packaged grocery store peppermint tea or, for that matter, *anything* we buy in the supermarket these days? It is mystery food. That's what we know.

But there are no questions, no concerns, no mysteries when I simply make my own peppermint tea.

My land was a former alfalfa field. I have grown food for myself and my family, and sometimes my friends, on this land for two decades. I do not use synthetic killing and fertilizing chemicals. I have been an organic gardener as long as I have gardened, more than 30 years. I was organic before organic was cool, before the government, that lackey of the industrial providers, decreed in 2002 that it owned the word organic. As it is now, only those who get permission from the organic bureaucrats can legally use the word.

So I picked my own peppermint that day and I piled the stems on a cookie sheet beside me. Before the leaves had a chance to even wilt, I had them in my Excalibur food dehydrator. I removed every other tray and packed the fresh stems in. I set the heat for medium. Within 24 hours, the peppermint was crispy dry. It was not cooked brown. It was still a pleasant green.

Once dry, I took the peppermint from the dryer and put it, stem and all, while still warm, into a half gallon, wide-mouth canning jar. You can pack a surprising quantity of dry herbs into a canning jar. I stored it in my cool, dark pantry. But not before making myself a cup of tea.

To make the tea, I withdrew a small bunch of dried peppermint leaves. I rubbed them between my hands over a plate to make small pieces. I pushed the pieces into a pile and used them to fill a stainless steel tea ball. I set the ball into a sturdy mug—it's bigger than a teacup and, frankly, more manly—and I filled it with boiling water. The water quickly turned an earthy greenish brown. Peppermint steam rose and I moved my nose down to meet it. The rich, powerfully-fresh, delicious aroma promised better things to come. And it kept its promise. The first sip of that tea was such a delight that I have been harvesting my own peppermint and making my own tea ever since.

It is ridiculously easy to grow peppermint. It is also easy to pick and dry it, even if you don't have an electric dehydrator. And, as I've pointed out here, homemade peppermint tea is, in every way, unquestionably superior to that supermarket stuff.

Nevertheless, relatively few people in our modern culture have ever made their own peppermint tea from their own homegrown peppermint. They would rather buy 20 already-made tea bags neatly arranged in a box for less than three bucks. If you are one of those people, I hope this story has inspired you to make your own tea. It needn't be peppermint. It could be any of a number of easily grown and excitingly delectable herbs that suit you. And your tea need not be consumed hot. A tall glass of iced peppermint tea on a hot summer day is heavenly.

The point of this story is that some of the greatest joys in life can come from the simplest of things . . . like, for example, a cup of tea you've grown and harvested yourself.

Simplicity is the ultimate sophistication.
—Leonardo da Vinci

You can never get a cup of tea large enough
or a book long enough to suit me.
—C. S. Lewis

28

My Mother

S HE WAS BORN INTO THIS WORLD ON AUGUST 10, 1936 in Fort Fairfield, Maine. Dr. Herrick Kimball performed the delivery. I know this because, years later, she married Dr. Kimball's son and then gave birth to me. I was named after my grandfather.

My mother and the doctor's son did not stay married long. A couple years after the divorce, she remarried and we moved to a little ranch house in Seneca Knolls, a suburban subdivision outside Syracuse, New York.

Divorce is difficult for any child. I've often thought it was less traumatic for me because I was so young at the time. But I was old enough to be confused and insecure about what had happened, and one day that insecurity bubbled to the surface. I must have been six years old at the time.

My mother was sitting at the kitchen table working away at something. I was standing near her. She was telling me that she and Dick (my new father) would be going somewhere the next day and a babysitter would be staying with me. I was concerned and innocently, sincerely, I asked, "Are you going to leave me too?"

She knew what I meant and responded immediately. My mother pulled me close and hugged me tight. With deep emotion, she said, "No. No. No. I'll never leave you, Herrick. You don't ever have to worry about that." It was what the little boy very much needed to hear.

Forty years later, April of 2002 to be exact, my mother called and asked me to come see her. She had something she wanted to tell me.

My mother and stepfather lived only three miles away, in the old farm house we had moved to when I was in ninth grade. I visited my parents regularly. But with three kids and my job, life was busy and I saw them less and less.

Visiting with my Mom was something I enjoyed. She was always so happy to see me, so encouraging, so interested in what I was doing and what I was thinking. That my mother was proud of me was evident. We talked about the family, about friends and local news, about American history and current events, about the problems of our decaying culture. We shared the same biblical worldview.

My mother was a Christian. Her faith was strong and deep and anchored on the solid rock. It was her influence in my life that led me to embrace her faith, to know God the Father through His son, Jesus Christ.

On that April day in 2002 when I went to visit my mother, we sat on the couch in the living room, and she told me that she had been diagnosed with cancer.

The news was a shock to me. Except for an occasional bout with cold and flu viruses, I had never known my mother to be sick. She did not look sick. She did not act sick. My mother had always been a picture of health.

We talked for a couple of hours. She reminisced about her life growing up, the youngest in a family of 10 children, on a potato farm in northern Maine. Life was not easy then. Her mother and father worked hard and struggled to make ends meet. They never had a lot in the way of material success. Nevertheless, my mother had fond memories of growing up on the farm. After we talked, we prayed together and I went home, wondering what the future would bring.

My mother refused to have surgery or take any kind of drugs. She had no faith in modern medicine when it came to curing disease. She felt that modern medicine only treated symptoms and doctors *practiced*; she did not want them practicing on her.

She had no regular doctor. She almost never went to doctors. She did not trust the doctor who diagnosed her. He wanted to start chemotherapy. She had known too many people who went through the hell of conventional cancer treatments, only to die a short while later.

My mother chose to put her faith in God instead of modern medicine. She believed that it was not God's will that any of His children be sick. She believed He would heal her. In line with this train of thought, she consulted with a naturopath. She would use herbs, vitamins, raw vegetable juices, and a host of other natural things to build her immune system and enable her body to fight off the cancer. Some people thought this was foolish. I was not one of them. It was my mother's choice and I supported her in it.

The months passed. She seemed to be doing well. Then she went into decline. At one point she became so weak that she was barely able to stand on her own. My dad called one day for help. Marlene and I rushed to the house. My mother, her skin so pale, was lying on the floor. My father had been helping her walk and her legs gave out. She was not distressed. She was calm. But she was weak and emaciated and helpless. She weighed less than a hundred pounds.

It was decided that we must take her to the hospital emergency room. Marlene helped bundle her against the cold autumn wind. I picked my mother up and carried her in my arms out of the house. I placed her in the back seat of my vehicle.

At the hospital they told us my mother had lost so much blood that, had we not brought her in, she would have died within a few hours. They gave her several units of new blood. She remained in the hospital a couple days before coming home. The transfusions made a big difference. My mother was like a new person. But only for a while.

Before long, she was bedridden. My father had a part-time job that required him to work some evenings. When he could not be with my mother, Marlene would be there. My sweet wife spent many hours tending to my mother's needs. I did what I could, but Marlene was the angel. She loved and cared for her mother-in-law like she was her own mother.

I visited my mother periodically in the evenings. Her bed was in a downstairs living room. We called it the "stove room" because there was a woodstove in there, making the room warm and cozy.

We talked and sometimes I would read to her from her Bible. She once asked me to read her Psalm 103. It begins:

Bless the LORD, O my soul: and all that is within me, bless his holy name. Bless the LORD, O my soul, and forget not all his benefits: Who forgiveth all thine iniquities; who healeth all thy diseases.

Later into the psalm, it reads:

As for man, his days are as grass: as a flower of the field, so he flourisheth. For the wind passeth over it, and it is gone; and the place thereof shall know it no more.

My Mom's health slowly, continually declined. Still, she trusted in God's healing. Friends and family called. They sent cards. Some brought meals. My two younger sisters came from out of state to visit for a time.

Before long, she talked less. She seldom opened her eyes. She showed little emotion except, on occasion, to wince in pain.

I had never before seen anyone slowly waste away and die, and here was my once-vibrant mother suffering unto death. I kept my composure when I was with her. But the tears flowed when I was alone in the car driving home. I prayed that the Lord would be merciful and take her soon.

One evening, around that time, alone with my mother, kneeling by her bedside, holding her skeletal hand in mine, I drew close and spoke quietly. She was lying on her back, her eyes closed. I asked her if she could hear me. She gave a slight nod.

I asked her if she remembered the time when I was a little boy and we had just moved to the house in Seneca Knolls and I asked her if she was going to leave me and she hugged me tight and assured me that she would never leave me.

Her face was expressionless but she gave another slight nod. "That meant so much to me, Momma. Thank you for loving me." I kissed her on the cheek and she gave my hand a squeeze.

A few days later, Marlene found a doctor who would come to the house for a woman who was not his regular patient. Marlene was there when he came. He said my mother was going to die very soon. He prescribed pills for the pain. He called hospice before leaving.

They showed up the next morning. A kindly woman came first and then a man arrived with a hospital bed. The stove room was a flurry of activity as we moved my mother's bed aside and set up the new hospital bed. At one point, my mother opened her sunken eyes and uttered the last words I ever heard her say: "Why are they trying to keep me alive like this?"

I answered: "They aren't trying to keep you alive, Mom. They're just trying to make you comfortable until the Lord comes to take you." I carefully lifted my mother from the sickbed into the new hospital bed.

Two days later, on March 17, 2003, eleven months after her diagnosis, sometime in the early morning, my dear mother passed from life temporal in this fallen realm to life eternal in a place where God's word tells us there is no sickness or pain or sorrow. In that instant, my mother received her healing.

I accepted my mother's death with resignation, thanksgiving, and praise. The Lord of all creation does as He pleases for his own *good* purposes. He does not need to justify his actions to anyone, least of all to me.

Life is not necessarily easy when you are a child of the King. Sometimes we must endure terrible hardships in this sin-corrupted world, but it is only for a season, and we are not left to endure it alone; He has promised never to leave or forsake us. That makes all the difference, and I rest assured in that promise.

My mother chose not to subject herself to the cold, cruel, procedure-driven monster of industrialized medicine. The industry exists primarily to make money, not heal bodies. That is what she believed. Some will agree with that. Most will disagree.

One thing is for certain, though. We will all die someday. And to die knowing a blessed eternity awaits you, to die in the peace and warmth of your own home, to die surrounded by a family that loves and cares and sacrifices for you, is not a bad way to go.

The sweetest sounds to mortals given
Are heard in Mother, Home, and Heaven.
—William Goldsmith Brown

A mother is the truest friend we have,
when trials heavy and sudden fall upon us;
when adversity takes the place of prosperity;
when friends who rejoice with us in
our sunshine desert us; when trouble
thickens around us, still she will cling to us,
and endeavor by her kind precepts and counsels
to dissipate the clouds of darkness,
and cause peace to return to our hearts.
—Washington Irving

I miss thee, my Mother! Thy image is still
The deepest impressed on my heart.
—Eliza Cook

29

Return of the Yeoman

THE AMERICAN SOUTH OF THE 1600s WAS AN agrarian culture with a three-tier class system. The ruling class, or aristocracy, was at the top. This included the wealthy landowners with large plantations, many of which contained thousands of acres.

Prior to around 1650, the aristocracy employed indentured servants to do their farming which was primarily tobacco. In exchange for passage to America, food, clothing, and a place to sleep, the servant labored for several years to fulfill the terms of his indenture. After that time, he was free to make his own way in the world.

England's demand for American tobacco, the scarcity of farm laborers, and the avarice of the aristocracy led to the introduction of slavery in America. Slavery replaced indenture. Slaves were more permanent help than indentured servants. It was the indentured and the slaves that made up the lower class of this early southern agrarian society.

Then there was the yeomanry, which was the large middle class of hands-on farmers, some of whom had once been indentured. The yeoman was a landowner, but his farm was not a vast plantation. Most yeomen started with 50 acres of land. A true yeoman was a freeholder, meaning he owned his land free and clear.

The yeoman's land was his earthly dominion; he was the king and husbandman of the realm. With the hard work of the yeoman and his family, the land provided virtually all of their needs and a cash crop to boot.

Yeomen were not known for extravagance or ostentation. They were simple people of the soil. With the money from their cash crop, they were able to purchase additional acreage. The acquisition of more land for himself and his children was a very important thing to the yeoman. In time, many yeomen had farms of several hundred acres and a measure of prosperity. But a true yeoman remained a simple-living farmer.

The farm of a typical yeoman was diversified with horses, mules, cattle, swine, and poultry of all kinds. There would be an orchard and a very large garden. Self-sufficiency was a hallmark of the yeomanry.

The skills of the yeoman were not limited to farming. He built his own house and barns with lumber from his own land. Many yeomen were smiths and could make their own tools. They built their own furniture. In short, the yeoman was a resourceful and multitalented person. The yeoman's wife was a picture of industry too. And his children, of which there would be many, were an integral part of the family economy.

The American yeomen were predominantly, but not exclusively, Christians and Protestant. Their faith was central to the way they lived their lives. They lived in close-knit community with their kin and others who shared their beliefs.

When the southern aristocracy began to import slaves from Africa, tobacco production increased and the price fell. This hurt the yeoman class. Many yeomen felt it was necessary to take on a few slaves. But yeomen did not own slaves like the big plantations did. And they typically worked alongside the slaves.

In the north, the yeoman farmer was characterized by the same qualities as his southern counterpart: land ownership, hard work, simple living, resourcefulness, self-sufficiency, and independence.

Because the yeoman understood what real freedom was, he was wary of government infringing on the inalienable rights he recognized as coming from his Creator.

It was a small group of yeomen on Lexington Green that, in the spring of 1775, stood its ground against a regiment of the king's troops on its way to seize the armory of nearby Concord.

After several of these brave yeomen were shot and killed that day, it was the yeomen of the surrounding countryside who, from behind the rocks and trees along the roadside, dogged, sniped, and killed the redcoats as they ran all the way back to Boston.

In the resulting War of Independence, it was yeoman farmers of the north and south who, under the leadership of the farmer-general, George Washington, did the fighting and dying. By the grace of God, those farmers prevailed against what was then the most powerful and professional military force on the face of the earth. Have you seen "The Patriot," starring Mel Gibson? In that movie, Gibson's persona is something akin to a southern yeoman.

Mel Gibson aside, the typical yeoman of America was not a warrior. He was a farmer and a family man. But like every true man, he had within him the heart of a warrior. That heart was moved to action by injustice and conviction and faith and duty. It's imperative to understand that the yeoman soldiers of the Revolutionary War were motivated by a sense of duty not only in the here and now, but for their posterity; they were fighting for the generations of their children whom they would never know. This is an example of multigenerational vision in action.

Thomas Jefferson, another farmer-statesman, had a vision for America that few people know about. Jefferson believed that the new form of government he helped to establish was best suited for, and would be best served and preserved by, a politically decentralized agrarian culture.

Jefferson believed the strong backbone of such a civilization would and should be the yeoman farmers. Because they were self-reliant and independent, they were beholden to none. They would therefore not be easily influenced by self-serving politicians who sell their votes (and their souls) to special interests while promising the world to their constituents.

Furthermore, Jefferson knew that men who lived simply and close to the soil were, as a rule, also men of virtue. The yeomanry would be yet another check against the overgrowth of a central government and the inevitable tyranny that results when government gets too big for its britches.

Unfortunately, Jefferson's vision was derailed by the industrial revolution. But that revolution, built as it was on greed, envy, idolatry, love of money, laziness, and irresponsibility is running out of fuel . . . literally.

The industrial revolution is in decline. Its days are numbered. We are entering a period of transition. For many it will be a time of confusion, hopelessness, and despair. It will be a time when God humbles the masses.

This is why I believe He is reestablishing a Christian yeomanry. He is calling many of His people to return to the land, to the soil, to build strong families, to build self-sufficient homesteads, to be good neighbors, to be salt and light to the community around them, to offer hope in the midst of turmoil, to reap the harvest in its season.

*The British soldiers were shocked.
These farmers had not scurried
away at the first volley . . . Here
they stood their ground and calmly
returned fire. And they could shoot!
As the first British squad knelt to
reload, the second took aim behind
them. At that instant the second squad
became aware that there was no third
squad behind them. The third squad
had run. Immediatly, the second and
first squads ran after them.*

—Peter Marshall and David Manuel
The Light and the Glory
(speaking of the first skirmish in the Revolutionary War)

118

30

My Son
and His Journal

I WANT TO SHARE WITH YOU FROM MY SON'S daily journal. But first, I will tell you a little about him and how he came to keep a journal.

His name is Robert E. Lee Kimball. Robert is 14 years old and almost as tall as his father. But, unlike his father, there is no extra fat on his body; he is all sinew and bone and heart. He loves the outdoors. He is mechanically minded. He has the hands of a craftsman. He is forever coming up with ideas for new things to build and, in many instances, actually building them. He is not hesitant when it comes to a physical challenge, even if it is in the form of work. He is, in other words, a quintessential country boy.

Robert likes to earn money, and he is a good saver. For the past couple of years he has been saving for a four-wheeler. He needs to earn and save the money because his father will not buy him a four-wheeler. The neighbor boys have four-wheelers that their parents bought for them. But Robert's father does not have the money to spare, and he surely won't go into debt for something like that.

So my son has been making money many different ways. With his mother's help he bakes and sells small loaves of zucchini and pumpkin bread at the farmer's market on Thursdays during the summer. Last year he worked many hot afternoons helping a local farmer get his hay into the barn. He mows his grandmother's lawn. He traps and shoots rats outside our chicken coop for the dollar bounty his mother gives him. He earned $75 from me last month for splitting ten face cords of firewood with a maul. He does odd jobs for neighbors whenever he can. And he writes in his journal. I told Robert I would pay him $10 a month if he wrote in a journal every day.

He started the journal 298 days ago. I know this because, along with the day of the week and date, Robert numbers each entry. The journal has now grown to four spiral note-book volumes. Each day's entry is on a single page. If he writes a lot, it continues on the back of the page.

Along with each entry is a drawing. Some drawings are silly faces in profile. Others are of animals he has trapped. One drawing shows our dog, Annie, barking at a snarling raccoon. The one I like best is of Robert and his little brother, James, standing under a wasp nest hung high up in a tree that's drawn as tall as the page. They are trying to knock the nest down and the bees are flying all around.

Robert's spelling is not the best, and his punctuation is often nonexistent, and his writing is rarely as neat as it can be. But the journal is not a school assignment that I am reading and grading on its technical merits. Such things are not important to me in his journal.

What is important is that he is thinking about his day and putting his thoughts into words. He is also diligent about journaling; no one is nagging him to stick with it. And he is creating a wonderful chronicle of his life that he can go back and enjoy reading. After 298 days he is already doing this. Perhaps his children will read it one day. Perhaps his grand-children will, too. Best of all, Robert is having a good time journaling.

The following entries have been edited by me to correct some spelling and punctuation. The wording has not been changed. I hope you enjoy this peek into my son's journal. I hope that maybe it will inspire or encourage you to do the same with your children. Or, perhaps, to do the same yourself.

#58

Today I woke up and went downstairs and ate breakfast. Then did school which was math, spelling, and English. We did some spring cleaning. We mopped the kitchen floor. Me and James went down to the creek and we caught a 31-to 33-inch-long snake.

#65

Today I got up and did school for awhile and I helped Annie catch rats under the shop. Me and James went fishing and I didn't catch any till James and Ryan left. Anyways, we fished for awhile and James caught one fish. Ryan and James got cold and went home but I stayed because now the fish would bite because James and Ryan were not there to make noise. After they were gone, I caught a fish. Then I went home and ate supper. After supper I sat on our porch and put some feed on the driveway so I could shoot the rats that tried to get the bait. I shot two. After that, I went to bed.

#102

Today I got up and did a little school . . . Then I went out-side and heard Annie barking so I ran over to where she was and she had treed a woodchuck. So I poked it with a stick and it jumped down right towards me. I jumped out of the way and Annie couldn't get to it because she got stuck in some bushes. Well, the woodchuck ran away and into a hole. When all that was over we went to my grandma's house so my mom could go to some book sale in Binghamton. . . .

#148

Today I woke up and did some reading on my book about Tom Edison. And I played with the neighbors awhile just carving wooden boats with our knives. After that I went home and I worked on my money box for awhile till the neighbors came up. Then we played with them until they went home because we had to eat supper . . . Then we went to bed.

#156

Today I got up and I helped Dad put tiles in the kitchen. And we also had some subs for lunch. Then I went to a farm and unloaded hay. We did 5 wagons. And then we went home and I went woodchuck hunting but didn't get any.

#180

Today I woke up and I went to work at the farm. We unloaded some wagons with oat straw. And when we were done I went home and the field across the road was being combined and I got a ride on it.

182

Today I woke up and I worked on my dam in the creek. And after that we went to church but mom didn't go because she didn't feel very good. Anyways, we went to church and we listened to the sermon and then we went home and we ate till the neighbors came up and then we went fishing in the creek. We were just walking and in a foot deep little pool I saw a trout. We went crazy. We tried catching it with our fishing poles but that did not work too good so somehow we got the idea that we would just catch it with our hands. It works. You just feel under the rocks and ledges and holes under the water till you feel it. Then you grab it and pull it out. It is one of the funnest things to do.

#200

Today I got up and I helped Mom make bread. Then we went to the farm market and we sold our bread. When we were done, we only had two loaves left. We went out to eat at a restaurant but I forgot its name. We went out to eat for helping Mom do work.

#221

Today I woke up and I checked my traps. I did not catch anything in the traps in the woods but I caught a skunk in the trap that I set in a field across the road. After that I did my school which was math, English, and spelling. When we got done with school, me and James went woodchuck hunting. James shot a woodchuck at 25 to 50 yards away, right between the eyes. We went home and James skinned the animal. Then we set a few more traps, then went to bed.

#224

Today I woke up and I didn't do very much at all. But we did butcher chickens.

#249

Today I woke up and did a little school which was the usual. After that I made some of my furniture, which is a firewood holder. After that we went to Moravia and got pizza and wings. Then we went home and ate it because it's James's birthday. After that we went to sleep.

#267

Today I woke up and I did school. Then we went to the animal clinic and got Annie a booster shot since she got in a scuffle with a 20 lb. coon. So we got that. Then I went with James and Chaz to basketball practice and we did our thing there. Then we went to bed.

#271

Today I woke up and I split some wood. Well, actually, the rest of the wood. Then we went to my grandpa's house and did a little work. Then we went home and did some other boring things. Then went to bed.

#272

Today I woke up and went to church. We listened to the sermon about giving and after that we stayed for the meal. After that we went home and a big storm with lightning and thunder and high winds knocked over our basketball hoop and a few trees. When that was over we went to bed.

#276

Today I woke up and read some of my book called *Farmer Boy*. Then the Rices came over to do unit studies. We learned about magnets and also about the smallest thing in the world, an atom. After we did that we played Jeopardy which was kinda fun. Then we played inside for awhile. Then they left and we went to bed.

#280

Today I woke up and we did school which was spelling, vocabulary, and math, and also English. Then me and James went outside and built some of our fort. We just put bark on the roof of it. After that I tried skinning a squirrel and stuffing it with cotton. Then me and James heard two beagles in a field and chased them for several miles because they were on the trail of something and running and barking wildly at something they were chasing. We didn't see what they were chasing but we saw them. But when they got a way ahead of us we could hear them fighting with something. Then they would run on so we would chase them and get about 50 to 100 yards away from them but they would be running. So we gave up because it was getting dark and the dogs were getting too ahead of us, and because we were running and getting tired. So we went back to the house and we ate supper . . . .

#289

Today I woke up and I didn't do very much till about 6:15. That's when we went to Pie and Praise at our church and we ate pie and we praised the Lord for what He did for us this year.

My son's childhood, as expressed in the pages of his journal, is typical of a homeschooled, Christian agrarian country boy. I can't help but wonder how Robert's journal would read if he were a typical public-schooled, urban boy. Perhaps I am inclined to wonder about this because I know, from my own early childhood, that the contrast between the two lifestyles is significant. In the end, I find myself once again praising God for the blessings of rural life and the fruit it bears.

31

Working in the Field with My Grandfather

M Y EARLIEST RECOLLECTION OF DOING physical work goes back to when I was seven years old, and I helped my grandfather on his farm. It is a memory I cherish.

His name was Percy O. Philbrick, and he was 69 years old when this story took place. My grandfather's lot in life had been that of a hardscrabble potato farmer in Fort Fairfield, Maine. It had not been an easy journey for him and my grandmother, Gertrude, living through the Depression and raising ten children on potatoes.

My grandparents were intimately familiar with hard, seemingly endless, often desperate work, and they knew, as only poor dirt farmers can, the heartache that comes with having labored so diligently and so hopefully, only to see it come to naught. Bad weather, potato rot, and punishingly low crop prices can, at times, conspire with such cruelty. There were also other character-building hazards of life, like sickness and the fire that burned their home to the ground in the winter of 1933.

But Percy and Gertrude were hardy people—they had no choice, really, but to be hardy—and the Lord blessed them. While they never accumulated an abundance of material possessions or a big bank account, those things by which the world so foolishly measures success, they did possess the plebeian wisdom, gentle humility, knowing patience, and grateful spirit that hardship and difficulty can cultivate in a life.

When my grandfather's heart, once so strong and dependable, finally failed him in the summer of 1971, he and Gertrude had been married 48 years, for better and worse, and they loved each other to the end. Furthermore, they had managed to hold on to the farm while so many around them had not.

All of that is part of my family history. It is why all of their children, and the many more grandchildren, like me, look back so fondly with their remembrances of that prim, wind-swept little farm.

Of course, none of this was a part of my consciousness when, in the summer of 1965, I was a skinny, freckle-faced, suburban, tract-house kid from upstate New York, visiting my grandparents for the summer. By then, Percy's hardest days were behind him. But still, like every old farmer, he loved to work the land and continued to do so even in his "retirement."

He was the son of a farmer, but none of his sons followed him. So, in his later years, my grandfather rented his land to a neighbor each growing season.

For the 1965 season, the neighboring farmer had planted sugar beets. Beets were something new in potato country. Evidently, they did not work out well because people no longer grow them up there. But I remember those beets. They were enormous!

Interspersed throughout the field were also large clusters of bright yellow mustard weed. My grandfather did not like the weeds in his field. My mother once told me that her dad had always been diligent about keeping his fields clean of the big mustard plants.

The time to pluck them was when they were in full bloom, before they had a chance to go to seed. That the crop was not his in that season of '65 made absolutely no difference to him. It was still his land and he intended to care for it as he had always done.

Driving his little gray and red Ford tractor with a flat wagon in tow, we slowly made our way through the field, stopping periodically to pull every mustard around us. I loved riding on the wagon (what little boy wouldn't?), jumping off, walking among the leafy beets, and grappling with those colorful intruder plants.

I remember many being almost as tall as I was, but I still managed to pull them out by the roots, just as Grampy explained to me that I should do. I can only imagine the pleasure that he must have gotten from seeing his young grandson help with such enthusiasm.

Before we started, the field was dotted with the rogue weeds. When we were done, I could clearly see the results of our labor. The field was clean. The mustard was piled on the wagon. I do not remember being tired. I remember being exhilarated because I had helped my grandfather and, together, we had done an important job.

At seven years old I experienced the satisfaction of working in the soil, of husbanding the land, of exercising dominion as God created men—and their grandchildren—to do.

I also learned that there were other, more tangible, rewards that came to the working man. When we went back to the house, my grandfather gave me a shiny new Kennedy half dollar. Later, when I went with him to the country store down the road, I had my own hard-earned spending money. It was a good feeling.

❦

My father, all my people, held that no one
had a right to merely cumber the earth;
that the most contemptible of created beings
is the man who does nothing. I imbibed the
idea that I must work hard. . . The whole
family training taught me that I must
be doing, must be working—and at decent work.
—Theodore Roosevelt

*Young people need something stable
to hang on to—a culture connection,
a sense of their own past, a hope for
their own future. Most of all, they need
what grandparents can give them . . . .*
—Jay Kesler

❦

*Children need not only mothers and fathers
who are dedicated to them but also older adults
who are invested in their lives. The people most
qualified to fulfill that responsibility are loving
grandmas and grandpas who are passionately
committed to their own flesh and blood . . . .*
—Dr. James Dobson
Bringing Up Boys

❦

*Having a loving relationship with a grandparent
makes children feel special. It builds their self-esteem
to know there is an extended family that loves them.
A sense of identity develops as children learn about
their roots. They discover that grandparents have
time to listen with interest, to play, to let them help
with "real work," such as cooking or gardening. In
quiet unhurried moments, questions about faith and
life are answered from the knowledge of experience.
In these ways grandparents pass on their faith in
God while helping build confidence and self-worth.*
—Karen Hart

❦

Elephants and grandchildren never forget.
—Andy Rooney

32

The Old Photograph

I N THE PREVIOUS STORY I TOLD YOU OF THE time I helped my grandfather pick the mustard weed from his field. Five summers before that, he and I posed for the photo that appears on the front cover of this book.

I'm certain my mother took the photograph. She was the one who gave it to me many years ago. It is the only photo I have of my grandfather and me. It is a picture that evokes my deepest emotions.

I see a lot of things in the old photograph. I see a little boy who loves being with his Grampy and an old man who delights in the company of his grandson.

I can also see what is not in the photo. I see the plain white farmhouse with its asbestos shingle siding. I see the big barn, the dark cavernous potato cellar underneath, the old farm implements out behind the barn, with their bouncy spring seats—the old bare-steel kind that were shaped to conform to your behind. I see my grandfather's lush garden. I see the raspberry patch that yielded such sweet fruit. I see white-blossomed potato fields, the cedar forests beyond, and so much more . . . .

I see myself shelling green peas with my grandmother on the stoop outside the kitchen door and eating so many raw ones that I got sick. I see my grandfather shaving with a straight razor in front of a round mirror at the kitchen table. I see my grandmother washing clothes in the back room with an old electric tub washer. It had casters on the bottom and a motorized wringer that I watched with rapt fascination as she fed soaking wet clothes into it.

I see the remarkable cantaloupes my grandfather grew— all the way up into the northern part of Maine! I see his chickens eagerly pecking the rinds when I threw them over the fence into their yard. I see the old folks, friends of my grandparents, who stopped by to visit. They seemed to know who I was but I had no idea who they were.

I see the boy running and exploring and playing. I see him digging for worms with his grandfather, going fishing and catching little brook trout. I see my grandfather chewing wonderfully fragrant wintergreen Skoal tobacco. All these things come into my mind's eye when I see the old photograph.

I can see my mother behind the camera. There is a smile on her face, the outward expression of the pride and joy she feels as she captures this treasured image of her father and her beloved firstborn child.

I see a man who is familiar and comfortable enough with the earth to sit himself down on it for a photograph. He was, after all, a man of the soil. I remember seeing him on his hands and knees, working in his garden. Unlike the industrialized farmer of today, who buys his food from a grocery store, my grandfather not only knew how to grow food for his family, he enjoyed doing so.

My grandfather appears to be suppressing a laugh in the photo. And do you see a hint of impishness in the little boy's smile? At two years old, the child has, no doubt, been an entertaining fellow. His soiled body and clothing are further evidence of his busy day.

The picture was taken in the late afternoon. I say that because Percy has slippers on his feet. I'd bet he was sitting comfortably in his rocker in the kitchen as he would do at the end of the day. My mother would have urged him outside for the photo. Conspicuously absent is the well-worn railroad engineer's cap that I remember him wearing.

My grandfather's arms are dark-tanned, as I'm sure they were all the summers of his life. They are strong arms. When he was a younger man, he cut firewood and sold it in town. That was back before motorized chainsaws, when men used bucksaws and muscle to get the job done.

My uncle, Clyde Kennedy, once told me that after the war, he finished building my grandparents' house which had been only partially rebuilt after the fire in '33. And he built the big potato barn, too. Uncle Clyde related to me that Percy was a powerful man and a *hard* worker. Clyde emphasized "hard" by drawing the word out when he said it.

Clyde told me that he had seen Percy lift 185-pound cedar barrels full of potatoes single handedly from the field up onto a flatbed truck. I have also heard that when the house caught fire, my grandfather threw the children out the door, then frantically ripped the large, heavy cast iron kitchen sink from the wall and carried it outside.

I wish that I could have known my grandfather better. But that I knew him at all was a blessing. His memory, the many little things I recall of him and my grandmother and their farm during the few childhood summers I visited, have impacted my life. They have inspired me more than anyone would have ever imagined.

Gertrude sold the farm shortly after Percy died back in 1971. She moved into a nice little apartment in a nearby town and has since passed away. The old homestead is now owned by people whom I do not know.

Several years ago, I flew back to Maine by myself for a brief visit. I made it a point to drive down Forrest Avenue Road, past the farm that had once been my grandparents'. I drove by very slowly, drinking it in. Then I stopped along the road in front of the barn.

The sign with the large, plain black lettering, *P.O. Philbrick*, that had been over the big doors in front of his barn, was long gone. The rusty farm equipment was gone. The raspberry patch was gone. But otherwise, the place I had known and loved appeared pretty much the same. This place held such wonderful memories. I sat in the car looking . . . and remembering . . . and I wept.

I marvel, not only at the provenance behind the old photograph, but at the Providence that prompted my mother to take it 46 years ago, preserved it so well, then directed it into my possession and finally, onto the cover of this book.

Is God so awesome that He can orchestrate the big events of history, like creating the world and all that's in it *and* guide all the smaller things too, like the daily lives and circumstances of men and women and little boys, even down to the taking of a simple family photograph?

It is difficult for my finite mind to fully grasp, but yes, I believe so, and I am thankful that it is so.

Thine, O Lord, is the greatness,
and the power, and the glory,
and the victory, and the majesty;
for all that is in the heaven
and in the earth is thine;
thine is the kingdom, O Lord, and
thou art exalted as head above all.
1 Chronicles 29:11

Afterword

I N THE FINAL ANALYSIS, AGRARIANISM APART from Christianity amounts to nothing special. But when individual lives that have been transformed by the power of Jesus Christ are imbued with the agrarian conviction, a fresh understanding and renewed sense of purpose emerges.

That has been my experience and this book has been, in part, my testimony. It is, essentially, a testimony to God's greatness and His goodness.

If my writings have entertained you, that is good. If they have encouraged you, that is better. If they have sparked a yearning deep within you, I urge you to put tinder to the spark and fan the flame.

Christian agrarianism is a great and noble and ancient adventure. Seek this good life with prayer, humility, wisdom, gusto, vigor, and resolve—and don't look back.

God bless you on your journey.

If you would like to contact me, my mailing address is:
Herrick Kimball, P.O. Box 1117, Moravia, NY 13118

If you would like to read more of my writings and
the writings of other Christian agrarians, I invite you
to visit my web site at:

www.TheDeliberateAgrarian.com

Whizbang Books
Down-To-Earth Inspiration and How-To Information

Whizbang Books is the home-based publishing company that I started back in 2002. The following three books are available directly from me. I'm not set up to take credit cards, but you can just send me a check or money order. Total up the cost of the books you want and add $3 for media mail shipping, or $5 for Priority. I typically ship orders out the day after I get them. Send your order to: Whizbang Books, P.O. Box 1117, Moravia, N.Y. 13118 If you have any questions, you can contact me directly by e-mail at: whizbangbooks@bci.net

Anyone Can Build A Tub-Style Mechanical Chicken Plucker

Hand-plucking chickens is nasty work. You can buy a mechanical plucking machine that does the job for you, but they are expensive. That's the situation that prompted me to build my own plucker. I didn't invent the plucker, I just figured out how to build one inexpensively, using commonly-available materials and basic handyman skills.

The thing worked so doggone good I called it the **Whizbang Plucker** and decided to put together a planbook telling other discouraged hand-pluckers how they could make their own miracle plucking device.

Homemade Whizbangs are now in use all across America and in several foreign countries. This plucker has made small-farm and backyard poultry production a whole lot easier.

The Whizbang will handle one to three chickens at a time and pluck them clean in 15 to 20 seconds. Pin feathers too! All you have to do is turn the machine on, drop your properly scalded birds in, and watch the show. You have to see it to believe it. The unit will also pluck a single turkey—up to 40 pounds—very nicely.

My plucker planbook tells you everything you need to know to build your own Whizbang, and it tells you where to get all the components. Once the parts are on hand, you should be able to build your own inexpensive plucker in a day, and it will faithfully pluck thousands of birds for years to come.

The planbook measures 8-1/2" by 11." It has 60 pages and 60 clear drawings. Price: $20.00

Anyone Can Build A
Whizbang Chicken Scalder

The most asked question I received from readers of my Whizbang Plucker planbook was, "When are you going to come out with plans for a Whizbang Scalder?" Well, it took three years.

Getting a good scald is the secret to fast, easy, and clean plucking. You can get a good scald with a pot of hot water over a propane burner (as I explain in the plucker book). But if you are processing a lot of birds as a business, a more efficient scalder is a tremendous asset.

An efficient scalder will heat up a tank of water relatively quickly, and automatically maintain a steady water temperature. My scalder design does just that. It begins with a common 40-gallon propane water heater. I tell you how to modify the heater to make a basic scalder, and how to work with the factory temperature controls to maintain a constant temperature. Then I tell you how to improve on the basic scalder by installing a digital temperature controller. The high-tech controller will *automatically* maintain the scald water within a 4-degree temperature range, which is ideal. Then, if you want to add more efficiency to the unit, I tell you how to install a motorized dunking mechanism. The "auto-dunker" will hold three chickens at a time and give you 120 chickens-per-hour capacity.

The Whizbang Scalder is designed to scald chickens only. It will not accommodate larger birds, like turkeys. But if you're handy you will be able to outfit a larger capacity turkey tank of your own design with a propane burner and control the water temperature with the same deluxe temperature controls I tell you all about in my planbook

As with the plucker planbook, this book tells you everything you need to know to build your own Whizbang Scalder, and it tells you where to find the harder-to-locate parts you'll need. Basic handyman skills and tools will do the job. Nevertheless, you should know that this project is not quite as easy as building your own plucker.

The planbook measures 8-1/2" by 11." It has 66 pages and 90 illustrations. Price: $23.95

The Complete Guide
To Making Great Garlic Powder

Most people in the world have never tasted homemade garlic powder. They think all garlic powder tastes like that stuff in the grocery store spice isle. Wrong. Store-bought garlic powder tastes like sawdust compared to homemade garlic powder.

I've been growing stiffneck garlic bulbs here on my homestead for several years now. And I even have a little home business making and selling "Herrick's Homegrown" stiffneck garlic powder.

Back in 2003 I decided to "write the book" on homemade garlic powder. With only 40 pages and 17 illustrations, it isn't a big book but it's packed with all the important details.

Chapter One introduces you to the "problem of grocery store powders" and reveals seven key elements of great garlic powder. In Chapter Two I share with you my special garlic growing techniques. In Chapter Three I explain the easy bulb-to-powder home processing system I've developed.

Homemade garlic powder doesn't just taste great, it's great for your health—and it makes great gifts too. Price: $6.50